Corporate Strategies of the Automotive Manufacturers

Corporate Strategies of the Automotive Manufacturers

John B. Schnapp
Project Director

Jennifer Cassettari
Research Coordinator

Project Team

Patricia A. Comer
Juergen Lange
J. Frank Remley, III
Hiroko Sakai
Jan-Hendrik van Leeuwen

Harbridge House, Inc.

LexingtonBooks
D.C. Heath and Company
Lexington, Massachusetts
Toronto

Library of Congress Cataloging in Publication Data

Harbridge House, Inc.
    Corporate strategies of the automotive manufacturers.

    Results of a study prepared for the National Highway Traffic Safety
Administration.
    Includes bibliographical references and index.
    1. Automobile industry and trade—United States—Management.
2. Products liability—Automobiles—United States. I. Schnapp, John B.
II. United States. National Highway Traffic Safety Administration.
III. Title.
HD9710.U52H32   1979   658'.92'920973   79-2788
ISBN 0-669-03243-3

Contents

List of Figures and Tables

Preface

The Energy Policy and Conservation Act of 1975 establishes "economic practicability" as one criterion for rule making. In our study for the National Highway Traffic Safety Administration (NHTSA), "Corporate Strategies of the Automotive Manufacturers," we have focused entirely on the economic sensitivities of major automotive regulatory programs. In doing so, we have neither questioned the public benefits to be derived from these programs nor endeavored to weigh those benefits against economic risk; rather, we have sought only to identify the character, magnitude, and likelihood of such risk.

The process undertaken by Harbridge House in its efforts for NHTSA involved the following major steps:

A historic review of the development of the strategies of the major automakers and of the economic dynamics of the automotive business

An investigation, through a wide variety of sources, of auto industry pricing policy, decision-making processes in the automotive companies, and the impact of automaker marketing efforts

Identification, with senior members of the NHTSA staff, of major economic externalities that could conflict with the principal federal regulatory goals

Analysis of these conflict scenarios

During this process which encompassed ten months, secondary research sources were invaluable. Nonetheless, our most important resource was a highly focused interviewing and data analysis program. The interviewing was done with executives of eight automotive manufacturing companies and numerous automotive industry experts outside these companies. Interactions with the automakers were voluntary on their part and were conducted under a uniform set of ground rules. Only one company and one individual refused to participate in our research effort; they are, respectively, International Harvester Company and Clarence Ditlow, Director of the Center for Auto Safety.

The conclusions we have formed are judgments of Harbridge House itself and are based on the totality of our research and analysis. We doubt if they coincide entirely with the views of any of our research sources, a predictable phenomenon in any subject area as complex and controversial as this one.

These conclusions, all related exclusively to the economic sensitivities of federal regulatory programs, are as follows.

1. The regulatory process and pace are accelerating structural changes in the automotive industry, largely by magnifying traditional economies of finan-

cial scale. This is likely to lead to an increasing concentration of market share by one or two of the largest companies.

2. The cost impact of regulatory standards, if passed through in automobile prices along with other cost increases affecting automobile production, is likely to create annual price increases that will exceed rates of inflation or growth in consumer income. If so, this may lead to the postponement of consumer auto purchases or to a "thrifting" of purchase patterns, either or both of which would diminish internal investment flows and thus adversely affect the capacity of U.S. automakers to generate the investment funds needed for regulatory compliance.

3. In the event of initial consumer resistance to new vehicle configurations, price increases influenced by regulatory costs, or corporate average fuel economy (CAFE)–related product mix goals of U.S. manufacturers, the marketing capabilities of the automakers can probably succeed in counteracting some resistance; but efforts to counter major resistance may result in a shrinking of profit margins and, with this, a shrinking of internal investment flows.

4. Even a minor recession in the next eight years is likely to destroy the abilities of Chrysler and American Motors to maintain their announced investment programs to meet already established regulatory requirements. A major recession, comparable to that of 1974-1975, or a second minor recession prior to 1985, would lead General Motors and Ford, between them, to raise approximately $5 billion of new capital simultaneously in a capital market of shrunken capacity. As a point of reference, the largest U.S. corporate borrower, AT&T, has never raised more than $1.569 billion at a single time.

5. The length of the product planning cycle has stretched to five or more years by the organic character of change required to meet regulatory requirements. Despite the efforts of the automakers to delay "point of no return" decisions as long as possible in the cycle, they are nonetheless making many basic decisions without the sort of confidence that a closer-in view of consumer interests and behavior would provide. This increases risks, especially for the smaller U.S. companies that cannot absorb any major product errors.

6. Current trends in the tort litigation system, working on the high expectations likely to be aroused by compulsory passive-restraint systems, will cause a considerably higher frequency of product liability suits to be launched against the automakers and, very likely, a higher product liability-related cost. The magnitude of this incremental cost remains virtually impossible to forecast.

7. Despite the dependence on a single technology (three-way catalytic converters) to meet 1981 emissions standards, despite dependence on the Republic of South Africa as the primary source of the catalytic metals, and despite a

mismatch between the natural occurrence of the metals and proportional requirements for them in the converter, it does not appear likely that either the technical or the political problems involved will interfere with the ability of the automakers to meet 1981 standards.

Part I
Future Scenarios

The National Highway Traffic Safety Administration (NHTSA) asked Harbridge House to investigate three specific "future scenarios" selected by senior members of the NHTSA staff. Each of these scenarios involves a major federal regulatory program in the passenger car field and an "environmental" counterforce, using *environmental* in the broad sense of identifying anything wholly external to the automotive industry.

The pairing of programs and counterforces selected was the following:

Program	Environmental Counterforce
Current and possible post-1985 fuel economy	Economic recession
Occupant safety under Motor Vehicle Safety Standard 208	Trends in product liability legislation and judicial interpretation
Emissions control	Interruptions or shortages in the supply of platinum-group metals

The intent of this effort was to assess the severity of the possible conflicts between the programs and the counterforces, the likelihood that such conflicts would emerge, and the public policy options available for dealing with them.

We chose to explore each so-called scenario both independently (that is, with experts outside the automotive industry) and with the eight major automakers on which our study focuses. As a result of this dual approach, we are reporting our findings in a dual way:

A Harbridge House overview of each scenario which represents our own summary thoughts on it, derived from both elements of our research.

A series of views expressed by each company of each scenario. These views reflect the direct commentary made by company executives of the impact of each scenario on their own company or our own synthesis of relevant company commentary and action. (It should be noted that in addition to the discussions of the individual Japanese automakers in terms of selected U.S. regulatory issues, some relevant aspects of comparable issues within Japan that can be generalized for the Japanese automotive industry as a whole are briefly described in the appendix.)

The company views on a single scenario reflect considerable diversity, not only of viewpoint but also of interest. We discovered that although certain aspects of a particular scenario might be of major importance to some companies, other companies proved to be relatively indifferent to them. Consequently, the company views reflect individual company interests as well.

1 The Impact of a Possible Economic Recession on Automaker Ability to Comply with Existing and Possible Future Fuel Economy Standards

Harbridge House Overview

Current Views of 1978-1985 Capital Investment Requirements

In June 1978 the Big Three automotive manufacturing firms—General Motors, Ford, and Chrysler—revealed to *Automotive News* estimates of their respective worldwide capital investment requirements for property, plant, and equipment (PPE) and special tools through 1985. As shown, two of these estimates differed significantly from those forecast in November 1977:

	Nov. 1977	*June 1978*	
GM	$31.5B	$38.0B	At approximately $4.0B per annum in 1978-1979 and $5.0B per annum in 1980-1985
Ford	$18.0B	$26.5B[1]	Budgeted $12.75B through 1981; probable additional $12.75B required for 1982-1985
Chrysler	Not announced	$ 4.75B[2]	At approximately $0.95B per annum through 1982; thereafter at approximately $0.5B per annum[2]

The sharp increase in the GM/Ford aggregate forecast in only seven months—a rise of 30 percent—is notable and probably reflects a growing sense of the cost and complexity of complying with fuel efficiency, safety, and emissions standards while still offering a product whose character and price remain attractive, in company judgment, to the public.

3

A look at derivative and/or unaudited data for the first quarter of 1978 reveals that none of the companies is yet quite on the investment "track" implied in the June announcements. General Motors' actual first quarter expenditures for PPE and special tooling seem to have approximated $850 million rather than $1 billion. Ford appears to have been undertaking new investment at about 65 percent of the level announced, and Chrysler at approximately 50 percent.

Despite the apparent evidence that the Big Three are not yet investing at the rate they have forecast, the June forecasts must be viewed as the most authoritative existing calculations of capital investment requirements for the 1978-1985 period.

Proportion of Investment Attributable
to Regulatory Standards

The historic investment patterns of the Big Three automakers typically show great variance from year to year, both in terms of total amount and in the relationships between PPE and tooling. This is evident in table 1-1 which shows the patterns for each company during the 1968-1977 period. This is caused in the PPE account by the tendency of many individual projects such as new production facilities or the reengineering of existing ones to represent large single amounts. In tooling, the introduction of a totally new model or even of a new body may, in itself, cause an apparent "bunching" of expenditures.

To gain some insight into long-term normal growth rates of investment, we developed five-year rolling averages for 1967-1976. Despite considerable investment in the years 1974 to 1976 related to regulatory standards, the annual amounts invested even in 1976 were not abnormal by prior standards. (The 1974-1975 recession did cause depressed spending levels in 1976. Therefore, in 1977, a high-profit year, investment spending was higher than in any prior period to an unprecedented degree.)

The secular rates of increase in worldwide capital investment during this more or less "normal" decade were as follows:

General Motors	Approximately 4 percent per annum
Ford	Approximately 5 percent per annum
Chrysler	Approximately 2 percent per annum

Using these "normal" annual percentage increases in worldwide capital investment on a compound basis with the actual 1976 investments of the three companies—$2.30 billion for GM, $1.05 billion for Ford, and $0.42 billion for Chrysler—we calculated a "normal" aggregate of worldwide capital investment for the 1978-1985 period to compare with the actual corporate forecasts. We

Table 1-1
Annual Capital Investments of the Big Three Automakers, 1968-1977
(millions of $)

	1968	1969	1970	1971	1972	1973	1974	1975	1976	1977	Total
General Motors											
Property, plant, & equipment	860	1,044	1,134	1,013	940	1,163	1,459	1,201	999	1,871	11,684
Special tools	866	863	1,149	631	899	941	1,096	1,036	1,308	1,776	10,565
Total	1,726	1,907	2,283	1,644	1,839	2,104	2,555	2,237	2,307	3,647	22,249
Ford											
Property, plant, & equipment	462	534	564	609	691	892	833	614	551	1,090	6,840
Special tools	417	424	484	430	463	594	619	342	504	673	4,950
Total	879	958	1,048	1,039	1,154	1,486	1,452	956	1,055	1,763	11,790
Chrysler											
Property, plant, & equipment	217	375	174	114	169	331	226	164	227	386	2,383
Special tools	205	272	242	136	166	298	242	220	197	337	2,315
Total	422	647	416	250	335	629	468	384	424	723	4,698

Source: Corporate annual reports, 1969 to 1978.

assume the difference to be primarily the incremental investment required for U.S. regulatory compliance. The totals are as follows:

	Forecast Investment 1978-1985	"Normal" Investment 1978-1985	Increment for Regulatory Compliance[3]
General Motors	$38.00B	$23.0B	$15.00B
Ford	26.50B	11.2B	15.30B
Chrysler	6.25B	3.8B	2.45B

These rough estimates of regulatory increments may be somewhat understated. Because of expected tightness in capital availability, it is likely that all three companies are forgoing investment projects that would be undertaken under "normal" circumstances in favor of projects related to regulatory requirements.

*Automotive Investment as a
Public Policy Issue*

Under the Energy Policy and Conservation Act of 1975, the National Highway Traffic Safety Administration is enjoined to consider economic practicability as one criterion in its rule-making formulation and implementation. Under this structure, we believe that NHTSA must explore three major questions:

1. Assuming no abnormal shifts in the shape of the automotive business or the economy, would the automakers be able to generate the investment funds required to meet existing regulatory standards?
2. What would be the likely impact of a major economic downturn on their ability to generate the requisite funds?
3. If it appears unlikely that one or more of the major companies would be able to generate the necessary funds, either under normal economic conditions or if confronted with an economic downturn, what policy options would be open to NHTSA?

All three questions are rooted in existing regulatory standards which, in the case of fuel efficiency, encompass a period that stretches out to 1985. Both automakers and NHTSA officials, however, are looking beyond 1985. Should fuel efficiency standards, in particular, continue to be advanced in the years subsequent to 1985 and, if so, at a pace comparable to that currently embodied in the law? And if they are, would the necessary investments be within the possibilities of the automakers, again both under relatively normal economic conditions and in the event of a major downturn?

We believe that the farther questions—the hypothetical post-1985 ones—can best be addressed through the nearer ones. In other words, if it appears that the automakers can meet their investment requirements out to 1985, even under recession conditions, it would at least be likelier that they could do so after 1985 as long as the following conditions hold:

The post-1985 fuel economy standards are no more severe technologically and financially than the pre-1985 ones.

The automakers are not obliged to contend with any other standards of comparable technological and financial magnitude.

There are no major dislocations in the economics of the automobile business.

Therefore, we have chosen, both in our overview analysis and in our research with the principal automakers, to focus primarily on investment feasibility and sensitivity out to 1985, assuming this period to be the best available guide to the post-1985 period. It should be pointed out, however, with respect to the first condition, that most sources believe each successive increment in fuel economy achievement is likely to involve a geometric sort of investment increment.

A "Normal" View

We have taken the investment estimates made by the Big Three automakers in June 1978 and developed for each company a "normal" view of internal generation of capital (see tables 1-2, 1-3, and 1-4). In these views, each with its underlying assumptions, we have restricted ourselves to the primary sources of cash flow (net profit, depreciation of PPE, and amortization of special tools) and the primary uses (capital investments in PPE and special tooling, dividends, and increases in working capital).

Five broad assumptions are present in all three projections:

1. An average of the financial results achieved by the companies in 1976-1977 can be used as a base year for profitability.
2. There will be a secular upward trend in revenues and profits for all companies of 8 percent per annum, most of it (5 to 6 percent) inflationary and the remainder real growth.
3. Profit margins of the companies will remain unchanged at the 1976-1977 levels.
4. Market shares and mix will also remain largely unchanged.
5. There will be no recession. This is not to suggest that it would be "normal" for the United States to go through an eight-year period without a recession, but rather to provide a base against which the impacts of recessions of different magnitudes can be examined.

Table 1-2
Projection of General Motors' Capital Flows under "Normal" Circumstances, 1978-1985
(billions of $)

	Capital Need[a]	Profit	Less: Dividend	Net	Depreciation	Amortization	Total	Annual Variance	Cumulative Variance
1978	4.40	3.35	2.01	1.34	1.2	1.6	4.14	(0.26)	(0.26)
1979	4.40	3.62	2.17	1.45	1.2	1.6	4.25	(0.15)	(0.41)
1980	5.40	3.91	2.35	1.56	1.5	2.0	5.06	(0.34)	(0.75)
1981	5.45	4.22	2.53	1.69	1.5	2.0	5.19	(0.26)	(1.01)
1982	5.45	4.56	2.74	1.82	1.5	2.0	5.32	(0.13)	(1.14)
1983	5.50	4.92	2.95	1.97	1.5	2.0	5.47	(0.03)	(1.17)
1984	5.50	5.31	3.19	2.12	1.5	2.0	5.62	0.12	(1.05)
1985	5.55	5.73	3.44	2.29	1.5	2.0	5.79	0.24	(0.81)

Source: Harbridge House calculations.

General Motors Assumptions

1. *Profit:* $3.1 billion used as base is average of net profits in 1976 and 1977.

2. *Dividend:* Rate of 60 percent payout is slightly higher than 1976-1977 average of 57 percent but below ten-year average of 66 percent.

3. *Investment split:* Maintenance of traditional 50/50 split between PPE and tooling.

4. *Depreciation:* Large, continuous, and growing increments of investment will keep annual depreciation at approximately 60 percent of annual investment, down from nearly 70 percent range of past five years. This is a deliberately conservative estimate.

5. *Amortization:* Large, continuous, and growing increments of investment will keep annual amortization at approximately 80 percent of annual investment, down from 95 percent range of past five years. This is a deliberately conservative estimate.

6. *Total:* No deferred income tax or "other" included in total.

[a]Includes 5 percent per annum increase in working capital.

Table 1-3
Projection of Ford's Capital Flows under "Normal" Circumstances, 1978-1985
(billions of $)

	Capital Need[a]	Profit	Less: Dividend	Net	Depreciation	Amortization	Total	Annual Variance	Cumulative Variance
1978	3.34	1.62	0.57	1.05	1.02	1.00	3.07	(0.27)	(0.27)
1979	3.35	1.75	0.61	1.14	1.02	1.00	3.16	(0.19)	(0.46)
1980	3.35	1.89	0.66	1.23	1.02	1.00	3.25	(0.10)	(0.56)
1981	3.36	2.04	0.71	1.33	1.02	1.00	3.35	(0.01)	(0.57)
1982	3.37	2.20	0.77	1.43	1.02	1.00	3.45	0.08	(0.49)
1983	3.38	2.38	0.83	1.55	1.02	1.00	3.57	0.19	(0.30)
1984	3.39	2.57	0.90	1.67	1.02	1.00	3.69	0.30	—
1985	3.40	2.78	0.97	1.81	1.02	1.00	3.83	0.43	0.43

Source: Harbridge House calculations.

Ford Assumptions

1. *Profit:* $1.5 billion used as base is average of actual 1977 net profit plus actual 1976 net profit plus Ford estimate of $350 million in profit lost in 1976 because of a strike.

2. *Dividend:* Rate of 35.0 percent is higher than 1976-1977 average of 23.5 percent but lower than ten-year average of 39.0 percent.

3. *Investment split:* In accord with average maintained during past ten years and the most recent two years; 58 percent for PPE and 42 percent for tooling.

4. *Depreciation:* Large, continuous increments of investment will keep annual depreciation at approximately 55 percent of annual investment, down from 70 percent range of past five years and typically slightly below GM's. This is a deliberately conservative estimate.

5. *Amortization:* Large, continuous increments of investment will keep annual amortization at approximately 75 percent of annual investment, down from approximately 80 percent range of past five years and typically slightly below GM's. This is a deliberately conservative estimate.

6. *Total:* No deferred income tax or "other" include; in total.

aIncludes 5 percent per annum increase in working capital.

Table 1-4
Projection of Chrysler's Capital Flows under "Normal" Circumstances, 1978-1985
(billions of $)

	Capital Need[a]	Profit	Less: Dividend	Net	Depreciation	Amortization	Total	Annual Variance	Cumulative Variance
1978	$1.00	(0.12)	0.03	(0.15)	0.28	0.31	0.44	(0.56)	(0.56)
1979	1.01	0.30	0.08	0.22	0.28	0.31	0.81	(0.20)	(0.76)
1980	1.01	0.32	0.08	0.24	0.28	0.31	0.83	(0.18)	(0.94)
1981	1.01	0.35	0.08	0.27	0.28	0.31	0.86	(0.15)	(1.09)
1982	1.01	0.38	0.09	0.29	0.28	0.31	0.88	(0.13)	(1.22)
1983	0.57	0.41	0.09	0.31	0.28	0.29	0.88	0.31	(0.91)
1984	0.57	0.44	0.10	0.34	0.28	0.27	0.89	0.32	(0.59)
1985	0.58	0.48	0.10	0.38	0.28	0.23	0.89	0.31	(0.28)

Source: Harbridge House calculations.

Chrysler Assumptions

1. *Profit:* $300 million used as base beginning in 1979 is approximate average of net profits in 1976 and 1977 and also approximates average 1973-1976 earnings from continuing operations; loss of $120 million for 1978 is actual Chrysler forecast.

2. *Dividend:* Rate of 15 percent on common stock is slightly higher than 13 percent paid in the past two years; no common stock dividend assumed for 1978. Includes dividend on preferred stock.

3. *Investment split:* Maintenance of same split as Chrysler average for five-year period from 1973 to 1977 which was also reflected in actual 1977 investment split; 54 percent for PPE and 46 percent for tooling.

4. *Depreciation:* Large, continuous increments of investment until 1982 will keep annual depreciation at approximately 55 percent of annual investment, down from 60 percent range maintained in the 1973-1977 period. The same annual depreciation will probably continue in 1983-1985 despite lowered annual investments. This is a deliberately conservative estimate.

5. *Amortization:* Large and continuous increments of investment until 1982 will keep annual amortization at approximately 70 percent of annual investment, down from 75 percent range of past five years. The 70 percent figure is similar to past Chrysler experience for years in which the company's investment in tooling was increased substantially. As investment declines for the years 1983-1985, annual amortization will trail gradually downward. This is a deliberately conservative estimate.

6. *Total:* No deferred income tax or "other" included in total.

aIncludes 5 percent per annum increase in working capital.

All these have severe sensitivities, but none so much as the two that relate to profit levels. For example, by general agreement 1976 and 1977 were somewhat better than truly average years and were certainly enhanced by purchases postponed during 1974 and 1975. Margins, which had been undergoing a gradual secular decline since the mid-1960s, firmed in 1976 and 1977. Therefore, the profit components of our projections may reflect a somewhat optimistic view.

Under these "normal" circumstances and assumptions the following conclusions emerge:

General Motors. The company would have to generate approximately $1 billion of additional capital. It should have the ability to do so without major difficulty.

Ford. It would face a medium-term capital need of slightly more than $0.5 billion, peaking around 1980-1981. Although a large sum, this would appear to be easily within the company's capability. At the end of 1977 Ford held $1.9 billion of marketable securities. During 1974 it borrowed $560 million short term and an additional $500 million long term.

Chrysler. It appears to be facing a need for nearly $1.25 billion of incremental capital, peaking in 1982. The company's current preferred stock and warrants offering will generate approximately $300 million if the warrants are exercised. Chrysler's increase in equity can be expected to also increase its debt capacity so that the total inflow of capital, again assuming the exercise of warrants, could prove to be in the range of $450 million to $500 million. To meet its apparent capital needs, Chrysler would probably have to maintain its profitability, sustain a dividend in 1976-1977, and repeat its current capitalization effort once again before 1982. Failing this, its only apparent ready sources of incremental capital are its dividend and any marketable assets, for example, its shareholdings in offshore affiliates and subsidiaries.

Impact of a Recession

The two essential difficulties in viewing the impact of a possible recession on the capital investment generation of the Big Three automakers are defining the recession and calculating its magnitude for each automaker.

Defining the Recession. We believe it most reasonable and reliable to define a recession empirically as what happened to the automakers in 1974 and 1975. This has two great advantages. First, 1974 and 1975 served a major blow to the automakers in terms of both the magnitude and the length of the recessionary impacts. Passenger car registrations declined 22 percent in these two years over the prior two-year period. Second, the 1974-1975 period is recent enough that the financial impact experienced by the Big Three would seem to provide the most reliable, least hypothetical base for future estimates.

Calculating Its Magnitude. We chose the following method to estimate the cost of the 1974-1975 recession to each firm in profit dollars. First we took as our "normal" profit levels the same ones, based on 1976-1977, that we employed in developing our "normal" capital projections for the future. Then we reduced them by 8 percent per annum to convert them to "normal 1975" and "normal 1974" levels. This, for example, downgraded our GM 1976-1977 "normal" profit of $3.1 billion per year to $2.85 billion for 1975 and $2.62 billion for 1974. Next we subtracted actual corporate profits for 1974 and 1975 from our "normal" profit estimates. We believe that the differences represent a reasonable estimate of the cost of a recession like the one in 1974-1975 to each automaker in terms of lost net profit. The results were as follows:

General Motors	$3.29 billion
Ford	2.00 billion
Chrysler	0.84 billion

The future cost to each automaker of a 1974-1975 sort of recession will, of course, grow. To obtain a view of future impact, we compounded the 1974-1975 estimates by the same 8 percent per annum factor employed earlier in forecasting earnings growth. This seems reasonable since the same sorts of factors, notably inflation and real growth, which can be expected to make earnings grow will also have comparable downside effects in a recession. Our calculations of the cost to each company of a 1974-1975 sort of recession in each pair of years out to 1984-1985 is shown in table 1-5.

In comparing these sorts of recession impacts with our "normal" view of capital investment generation, we see the following:

General Motors. The company would be seriously affected. Nonetheless, if forced to compensate for the earnings lost in a severe recession, it could probably do so through debt without raising its ratio of long-term debt to equity much above 25 percent.

Ford. It would be very seriously affected and forced to undertake an unprecedented effort involving, quite probably, a combination of the issuance of new stock, incremental debt, and reduction of dividends. In a depressed capital market this may be difficult to accomplish, even for a company of Ford's size and financial strength.

Chrysler. A severe recession would be likely to destroy any possibility that Chrysler might maintain a capital program of a sort depicted in our "normal" view. To do so would require exceptional stability in its own profits as well as in the external environment. A severe recession would more than double Chrysler's need for external capital while simultaneously creating conditions that would make normal access to capital considerably more difficult.

Conclusions

Our "normal" projections are intentionally simplified. Apart from the use of a constant measure of inflation and real growth, they do not project any of the typical annual shifts in demand and profitability. They make no provision for strikes, although it has been more common than not for one of the automakers to be struck every three years. Above all, there are many ifs involved in them:

If the June 1978 investment forecasts of the Big Three automakers prove reasonably accurate

If there are no changes in federal or state rule making

If there are no major alterations in the economics of the auto business

If there is no large shift in market shares, in product mix at each company, and in the overall mix of consumer purchases

If profitability can be maintained at 1976-1977 levels

If profits grow at about 8 percent per annum, most of this growth inflationary but 2 percent to 3 percent of it real

If dividend policies do not change radically from current ones

Should all these ifs hold, at least in the aggregate, Chrysler Corporation would still find itself under "normal" circumstances with a severe capital

Table 1-5
Estimated Negative Impact of a Two-Year Recession Similar to 1974-1975 on Two-Year Net Profits of the Big Three Automakers, 1975-1976 to 1984-1985 *(billions of $)*

	General Motors	Ford	Chrysler
1975-1976	3.55	2.16	0.91
1976-1977	3.83	2.33	0.98
1977-1978	4.14	2.52	1.06
1978-1979	4.47	2.72	1.14
1979-1980	4.83	2.94	1.23
1980-1981	5.22	3.18	1.33
1981-1982	5.64	3.43	1.44
1982-1983	6.09	3.70	1.56
1983-1984	6.58	4.00	1.68
1984-1985	7.11	4.32	1.81

Source: Harbridge House calculations.

shortage and would find it extremely difficult to meet that shortage. Even if it succeeded in filling its capital needs under "normal" circumstances, it would still have to be very lucky or skillful to avoid a steadily deteriorating competitive position. With its two major competitors, respectively, investing five to eight times as much in the accelerated development of new models, it is difficult to imagine the maintenance of a stable, competitive framework.

But beyond this, it would seem totally improbable that there would be any period as long as eight years without at least one economic recession.

One "minor" recession, say *half* the magnitude of the one we have quantified, could probably be absorbed by General Motors and Ford by drawing on their cash and marketable security resources with some reinforcement of medium-term borrowing. The impact on Chrysler, however, would be catastrophic.

A second "minor" recession of this sort occurring, for example, in the early to mid-1980s, would confront GM with the need to find an additional $3 billion of capital and Ford nearly $2 billion at the same time. Two measures of the magnitude of such an undertaking are the following: The largest single medium- to long-term capital raising ever attempted by GM was $750 million; Ford's was $500 million. The largest borrowing ever undertaken by AT&T was $1.569 billion in 1970 for which it paid 8.75 percent, the highest interest rate ever encountered by that firm.

A scenario of this sort, that is, one in which there may be two "minor" recessions in the next eight years, does not seem unlikely. There have, for example, been two recessions in the last eight years. Should it be played out, the U.S. automotive industry, operating under the current regulatory standards, would likely be subjected to two vast aspects of change. First, its competitive framework would be radically and permanently altered, and it would become more highly concentrated. Short-term dislocations accompanying this change would probably affect the interests of significant numbers of the 800,000 employees identified by the Bureau of the Census as being involved in U.S. passenger car manufacture as well as the interests of the many employees of those supplier firms which, cumulatively, contribute more than 50 percent of the final value to the completed product.

The financial structures of the largest corporations would be altered considerably, their annual costs for new debt service would increase some $200 million to $300 million per year, and they would place unprecedented pressure on the capital markets at a time when those markets would likely be suffering from limited capacity.

Public Policy Options

In exploring the likely impact of a major recession or even a "minor" one on the ability of the Big Three automakers to comply with existing or possible future regulatory standards, there are several obvious options. Assuming the current structure of rule-making, the following seem the most evident:

Unwavering enforcement of established standards. This option would likely result in a major reshaping of the competitive structure of the auto industry and make it more highly concentrated. It would also be likely to cause vast short- to medium-term dislocations.

Relaxation of standards on a company-by-company basis. Essentially the formula pursued with respect to International Harvester on light truck fuel economy standards, this appears to be a pragmatic solution but one that probably raises legal questions of equity.

General moratorium on the enforcement of standards. This option has the limitation of gearing national interest goals such as fuel economy to the pace of the financially weakest firm.

The shortcomings evident in all three options may point toward the possible advantages of a different regulatory framework, one working through some combination of much higher fuel prices, less demanding minimum standards, weight-based vehicle taxation, and reliance on market mechanisms.

American Motors Corporation

The financial future of American Motors Corporation (AMC) as a vehicle manufacturer is tied more closely to its market share than to any possible shifts in the economy as a whole. Because most of its current passenger car models were developed several years ago and would have to compete with newly developed products, the company needs to substantially alter its product line if it wants to remain competitive and meet corporate average fuel economy (CAFE) standards. For example, the Pacer, which was developed before the energy crisis and with an emphasis on roominess and comfort rather than fuel economy, is considered a fuel-inefficient vehicle and thus has never been fully accepted in the marketplace. The Gremlin and the recently introduced Concord are both derivatives of the Hornet, which dates back to 1969. The shortcomings of the AMC product line have been heightened by the rapid pace of competitive new product introductions.

In recent years AMC has become increasingly dependent on Jeep sales for its corporate volume and profits. From 1975 to 1977 Jeep sales increased from 104,000 to 153,000 units while their portion of corporate revenues almost doubled, going from 21 to 40 percent. Thus, there is no doubt that Jeep vehicles have been essential to AMC's survival. Recent regulations on light trucks, however, force AMC to improve the fuel economy of its Jeep line if it wants to continue producing these vehicles. Consequently, AMC's first priority is to alter its Jeep line to comply with safety, emissions, and fuel economy regulations; it will cost AMC an estimated $100 million to develop a successor to the small CJ Jeep model. Reportedly, the company's next priority will be alteration of the Wagoneer line.

The management of AMC has repeatedly professed its intent to stay in the passenger car business. To meet CAFE standards, the company has had to find lighter, more economical engines and has had to develop lighter car bodies. Starting in 1980, AMC will purchase a new 2.5-liter four-cylinder engine from Pontiac to solve the first problem. This decision will allow the company to improve the efficiency of its engine line without having to invest in the development of a new drive train. However, it still leaves the company with substantial car body development work.

The average annual cash flow of AMC over the last eight years was $53 million. If this average holds, it is unlikely that the company will be able to finance the development of a new Jeep line out of retained earnings and amortization/depreciation alone. As for improvement of its passenger car line, it will clearly have to rely on outside help. In recent years AMC's debt-equity ratio has remained relatively low compared to the other financially troubled company, Chrysler. This would seem to allow the company to take on more long-term debt; however, because of the financial community's low confidence in AMC, expressed through relatively high interest rates on AMC's debt placements, it is extremely unlikely that the company could do so. For similar reasons a stock issue by AMC would have little chance of success, at least in the near future.

Apart from its recent decision to purchase engines from GM, AMC has taken two more steps to ensure the survival of its car business. First, it has started negotiations with the federal government on loan guarantees that would enable the firm to place up to $100 million in debt at normal interest rates. The proceeds could be used to improve the fuel efficiency of the Jeep line and keep this backbone of AMC's business competitive. Second, in March 1978 the company announced an intended arrangement with Renault under which AMC dealers would start distributing Renault's minicar at the end of 1978; and, more important for AMC, Renault's R-18 model would be considered for assembly in AMC's Kenosha, Wisconsin, plant. This will provide AMC with a compact, fuel-efficient family sedan without the company's having to invest heavily in research and development. However, to tool up the Kenosha plant for the assembly of Renault vehicles, AMC will still require large capital investments for which it will probably have to rely on Renault. Part of the current negotiations between the two companies appears to focus on the question of whether and to what extent Renault is willing to provide such capital.

Chrysler Corporation

During the 1978-1982 period Chrysler expects to spend $7.5 billion to develop and introduce in the United States new products that comply with federal fuel economy standards and to convert its domestic production apparatus. Approximately half of this total, $3.75 billion, will represent capital investments in plant, equipment, and special tooling. The remaining dollars will be used for ordinary business expenses, such as research and development (R&D) and start-up operations. During this same period Chrysler expects to spend $1 billion in capital expenditures in its European operations.

Chrysler intends to finance about two-thirds, or $3.16 billion, of its capital investments in the United States and Europe through amortization and depreciation. It believes that the balance, $1.59 billion, will have to be covered through new stock issues, new debt, and retained earnings.

In the first half of 1978, Chrysler successfully offered 10 million new shares of preferred stock at $25 each at an annual dividend of 11 percent. In addition, each share carried a one-half warrant to purchase a share of common stock for $13. Through this offering Chrysler raised $235 million net of a brokerage fee of $15 million. Exercise of the warrants may increase Chrysler's equity by another $65 million. Further, Chrysler expects that it could raise up to $250 million from the proceeds of its employee stock purchase plan. This leaves a total of approximately $1 billion more for Chrysler to raise in the next five years.

In assessing Chrysler's ability to finance the investments needed to comply with existing regulatory requirements, two critical areas should be addressed: Chrysler's ability to raise more capital and generate earnings.

Chrysler could raise its debt-equity ratio to 0.66 since loan covenants with Prudential Insurance and other major lenders allow the company to have a debt-equity ratio at that level. Consequently, $550 million of proceeds from preferred and common stock issues and from the employee stock purchase plan would allow the company to raise an additional $366 million in long-term debt, at least theoretically. However, the financial community's confidence in Chrysler has steadily decreased. Recently, Standard & Poor's lowered its rating of Chrysler bonds to BBB minus. It is therefore doubtful that in the near future Chrysler could raise anywhere near this amount of money on normal terms. A new debt placement would likely take the form of a five- to eight-year loan rather than the customary fifteen years or more, at an interest rate that would be substantially above the prime rate.

Even if Chrysler were able to place this much debt, it would still have to generate another $630 million. Additional debt would not be possible without another stock issue. Chrysler's recent issue of preferred stock was surprisingly successful, so much so that halfway through the issuing Chrysler expanded its offering from the original 6 million shares to 10 million. However, this offering required an unusually high underwriting fee and promised extremely generous terms to the new shareholders. Moreover, at a time when the market value of Chrysler's stock is only a fraction of its book value, any new stock offering would result in a serious dilution of owners' equity. It is therefore extremely unlikely that Chrysler would issue more new stock unless its profitability and stock performance improve.

Historically, the earnings of U.S. auto manufacturers have been a function of their size, with the larger manufacturers achieving higher profit margins than the smaller ones. Chrysler, with less volume and less vertical integration· than either Ford or GM, has not been able to achieve the return on sales of either of these firms in any one of the last twenty-five years.

Apart from its smaller size and lack of integration, Chrysler's profit margins have also suffered from manufacturing inefficiencies. Reportedly, Chrysler's direct manufacturing costs per vehicle have been 10 percent higher than those of GM. In the 1960s, under Lynn Townsend, chairman and chief executive officer, Chrysler gave priority to domestic and overseas expansion rather than improvement of the production apparatus. Under the team of John Riccardo and Eugene A. Cafiero, this policy was reversed so that one of their first objectives was to improve manufacturing efficiency. An example of this new strategy was the conversion of the Belvidere, Illinois, plant from the assembly of full-sized cars to the assembly of Omni/Horizon models. In the conversion virtually all the old equipment was removed and replaced by the most modern assembly and control equipment the industry can offer. As a result, the output of the plant has increased by more than 50 percent. Chrysler intends to continue this strategy by accompanying every new-model introduction in the coming years with a complete update of the plant in which that model will be produced. By 1982 Chrysler hopes to improve its manufacturing efficiency to the point where it is as close to GM's as it has ever been.

Whatever improvements Chrysler makes in manufacturing efficiency are likely to be offset to a great extent by the projected increase in expenditures required. From 1978 to 1982 Chrysler plans to spend close to $4 billion, or an average of $800 million per year, in North America on such expenditures as R&D and new product start-up. This is more than double the average of these expenditures in the previous five years.

Chrysler will also incur substantial increases in finance charges during this period. Yearly dividend payments on the recent preferred stock issue alone will be $27.5 million *after taxes*, or an equivalent of $40 million before taxes, assuming a tax rate of 30 percent. If Chrysler is able to place new debt, it will probably have to pay a substantial interest premium. Assuming a debt offering of $350 million at 11 percent, the company would face an additional interest expense of $38.5 million each year.

Considering these factors, Chrysler believes it unlikely that the company will be able to greatly improve its profitability record. The company has already announced a $120 million operating loss in the first quarter of 1978, and at best it expects to break even during the remaining three quarters. Therefore, any net profits and additions to retained earnings will have to come in the four-year period from 1979 to 1982. In this period Chrysler management states that anywhere from $400 million to $600 million will have to be generated from retained earnings to support its capital investment budget.

In the last ten years Chrysler's retained earnings have grown at an average rate of 5.8 percent. Assuming no further losses in 1978, the company's total retained earnings at the end of the year should be $1,764 million. Applying a growth rate of 6 percent to this base would produce an additional $463 million in retained earnings in four years. (It should be noted that by using a ten-year average the effect of the 1974-1975 recession on retained earnings has been somewhat smoothed out.) However, if a five-year average is used, this effect is much more noticeable. It shows the average growth rate of retained earnings in the last five years as only 4.8 percent. At that rate Chrysler would produce only $363 million in retained earnings during 1979-1982.

The previous considerations indicate that only under the most optimistic scenarios does Chrysler believe it would be able to finance its capital investment budget. This scenario assumes that Chrysler would be able to increase its debt to its maximum allowed debt-equity ratio and that through improved manufacturing efficiency it would be able to more than offset increased R&D, start-up, and finance costs, and thus improve its profitability compared to that of the past five years. However, if Chrysler should suffer the slightest reverse—for example, a slowdown in sales, whether accompanied by an economic downturn or not, or cost overruns, or tight conditions in the capital markets—it seems extremely unlikely that the company would be able to carry out its investment plans.

A question could be raised here as to how much Chrysler could reduce its investment program and how much money it could save or raise by dropping a model line or selling a subsidiary.

A substantial portion of Chrysler's capital budget is reserved for plant improvement and the acquisition of modern tooling and equipment. Thus, some savings could probably be made by ordering less advanced tooling and equipment. However, because advanced manufacturing equipment is essential for improving Chrysler's manufacturing efficiency, any cut in this part of the budget would have a negative impact on the company's profitability and thus its ability to finance the remaining portion of the budget.

In a nonregulated environment Chrysler would probably have been forced to concentrate on the most profitable segments of the market and abandon its strategy of meeting Ford and GM in all market segments. However, to meet the CAFE standards, the company has had to produce subcompact cars to offset the high fuel consumption of the larger, more profitable cars. The subcompact line clearly cannot be dropped. Dropping a full-sized car line would save investments, but it would also place Chrysler in a worse competitive position relative to Ford and GM, both of which have the resources to produce a complete spectrum of models. In addition, it would cost dearly in reduced corporate profitability.

During the 1974-1975 recession Chrysler reduced its operating expenses by severely cutting back its staffs. Most staffs have remained the same size since, except for manufacturing and engineering. Chrysler recently hired 1,000 new engineers, bringing back its manufacturing and engineering staffs to approximately the same size as before 1975. The company's inability to develop its own small engine, its delay in introducing the Omni/Horizon, and the quality problems surrounding these new lines can all be traced to its decision to reduce the number of engineers on staff. Therefore, it seems unlikely that Chrysler would resort to a similar cutback in a future downturn.

After years of losses or depressed earnings the fortunes of Chrysler's European subsidiaries seem to be improving. However, neither of them represents more than a small fraction of Chrysler's corporate assets, sales, and earnings. In January 1978 the market price of Chrysler's stock ranged between $11 and $12. With 60 million shares outstanding, the market value of the total Chrysler Corporation is between $600 million and $700 million. Therefore, it seems unlikely that the sale of a small fraction of this corporation could solve its capital problems.

Ford Motor Company

As already noted, Ford Motor Company recently increased its original estimate of worldwide capital investment requirements through 1985 from $18.0 billion to $26.5 billion (or more). Ford attributes this increase essentially to additional spending for regulatory compliance. This was due, first, to the company's misreading the U.S. Environmental Protection Agency's (EPA) definition of hydrocarbon emissions so that it did not include nonreactive methane in its calculations of hydrocarbon emissions tests (which was all right according to the definition under the Nixon administration) and thereby gained in fuel economy. Second, changes in regulatory testing procedures created the need for additional capital expenditures. (The methane issue affected only Ford whereas the testing affected all the automakers.) Of this $26.5 billion, some 30 to 40 percent will be allocated for overseas investments; at home Ford will spend $16.0 billion to $18.6 billion ($6.7 billion to $7.8 billion on special tooling and $9.3 billion to $10.8 billion on property, plant, and equipment) on facilities, machinery, and equipment for new-model programs, modernization, capacity additions, and productivity improvements. More specifically, this investment will most likely support the following programs (as well as others still to be announced):

Downsizing. In the 1978-1981 period Ford plans to reduce its corporate average fleet weight by 800 pounds.

Development of alternative engines, new engine capacity, and engine-related technology. These include new V-4s (2.3 liters); new 232 CID V-6s to be produced in the new Canadian plant by the 1982 model year; new V-8s (255 CID, 302 CID, and 351 CID); turbocharged and dual displacement engines; the PROCO engine; a diesel development program; and the Stirling engine (targeted for introduction in the early 1990s). Related to these programs are efforts to develop or improve new F10D transmissions, EEC III controls, engine modeling, three-way catalytic converters, fuel- and spark-advance technology, and so forth.

Manufacture of a passive-restraint system. Ford will probably second source with outside suppliers for an air bag system.

New-product development. These include the front-wheel-drive Pinto (Erika) for the 1981-model year, a new light truck (the Ram), and possibly an additional front-wheel-drive vehicle.

Because Ford is number two of the "Big Two," it sees itself in a position of having to compete directly with GM. Further, it believes that in order to do this, it must be a full-line company and cannot simply fill the niches and go after specific market segments. In addition, because the small cars necessary to meet CAFE standards are not highly profitable, Ford appears to believe that it has to invest in the upscaling of these low-profit products while producing as many higher-priced cars as possible. It feels that in this manner it will be able to maintain overall corporate profitability and thus generate internally as much of its capital investment needs as possible while continuing to maintain a stable dividend growth (40 percent payout). Implied in this strategy is Ford's current preoccupation with managing volume and product mix as well as its desire to expand capacity (and increase scale) to take advantage of opportunities created by shifting and growing markets. At the same time, Ford seems to feel that it must protect itself against economic environmental risks which could cause a major setback.

If Ford Motor Company is able to maintain its current performance (28.8 percent passenger car market share for the first six months of 1978, up from 27.6 percent in the first six months of 1977) and function within a "normal"[4] economic environment through 1985, it should be able to continue in a mode of "innovation," operating from a position of competitive strength vis-à-vis GM and gaining from its capital expenditures program in very significant ways. Moreover, if Ford's 1980 pilot program for the PROCO engine for full-sized cars (plus an oxidation converter) proves successful (which is still questionable, given some of the engines in mass production), this engine could be ready for production in the mid-1980s, giving the company an edge in the areas of CAFE and emissions control. This would also lessen Ford's dependence on the platinum-group metals, as discussed later).

Another opportunity that Ford can build on is the fact that it is traditionally stronger than GM in the small-car market. As the range of alternative configurations narrows and quality, performance, price, and the fuel economy of domestic cars and imports become similar, Ford believes it could be in an excellent position to gain market share. With a new upbeat 1979 Mustang/Capri product line, in addition to its new front-wheel-drive sub-compacts planned for the 1981-model year, Ford's relative small-car advantage should become even stronger.

Finally, Ford is a proved leader in the truck market. In Ford's view, this market has not yet reached saturation and represents another potential opportunity, especially with its new light truck line (the Ram) to be unveiled in the 1980-model year.

If, however, Ford is hit with a recession (in 1981-1982 or beyond) of the magnitude and duration of that of the 1974-1975 recession, or with two smaller recessions, one of which is coupled with a strike, then it would be hard pressed to meet all its obligations (to shareholders, regulators, the marketplace, and so on). For example, if it is assumed that a capital investment requirement of $26.5 billion through 1985 is adequate (especially in view of the fact that $12.75 billion is only an estimate for 1982 to 1985 and Ford seems to have a history of underestimating) and the estimated negative impact of a two-year recession (1981-1982 or 1982-1983, see table 1-5) is imposed, Ford's operating flexibility would be impacted significantly, making it difficult for the company to meet all its obligations.

In looking at Ford's history, several alternatives appear to be available to the company for raising needed capital:

The issuance of incremental long-term debt. Ford issued $229 million in 1970, $386 million in 1971, and $578 million in 1974 when its debt-equity ratio went as high as 24 percent. Its current debt-equity ratio is 16 percent.

The borrowing of additional short-term debt. Ford borrowed $500 million for its foreign subsidiaries in 1974.

A decrease in cash dividends. Ford has a tradition of stable dividend growth and has consistently maintained or increased its dividend rate, except in 1975 when the rate was decreased almost 20 percent.

A decrease in working capital. Ford decreased its working capital by $570 million in 1967, a strike year, selling off $488 million in marketable securities. It also sold $276 million in marketable securities in 1974. Ford currently has $1.9 billion in securities, having doubled this total in 1977.

The issuance of common stock. Ford seems to be in a good position to raise as much as $2 billion in needed capital by issuing approximately 45 million new shares of common stock (based on an average 1977 market price of $45). This would not significantly affect earnings per share (EPS). Based on

Ford's first quarterly report for 1978, EPS could be projected at $11.37 for 1978. This compares favorably with earlier strong performance years ($7.31 in 1973, $8.36 in 1976, and $14.16 in 1977—Ford's best sales year).

Assuming that all five options would be available to Ford and that all are viable, especially in light of Henry Ford II's visceral aversion to debt and desire not to dilute stockholders' equity, based on prior action Ford could probably raise as much as $3.5 billion of additional capital if it were willing to permit its debt-equity ratio to reach 25 percent and *if* the capital market could absorb a debt issue of mammoth proportions.

Ford's response to Harbridge House's "normal" view for the 1978-1985 period is that it is overly optimistic, that certain assumptions are not congruent with its own corporate objectives, and that other factors need to be considered.

1. Historically, the United States is hit with a recession every five years (on average). Therefore, there could be two recessions between now and 1985. Security analysts are currently forecasting an economic downturn for 1979-1980 and are incorporating this into their market analyses. Given such an occurrence, Harbridge House's net income trend line is overly optimistic, and as much as $6.74 billion higher than Ford's own projections over the 1978-1985 period.

2. Ford is likely to be the target company of the United Automobile Workers (UAW) in either the 1982 or the 1985 labor negotiations and may be struck. This, coupled with one or two moderate recessions, would seriously affect Ford's baseline profitability as well as its ability to raise necessary capital in either debt or equity markets.

3. The use of 1976-1977 as a base period for projecting profits is not reasonable in view of the fact that these were better than average years for Ford.

4. Ford's profits in 1974 and 1975 were "inflated" since the company deferred highly desirable future-oriented cost-cutting and/or profit-producing programs in those years. This is significant from two viewpoints: Ford is currently experiencing a loss of revenues (opportunity costs) that would have been generated by these programs, and current/future capital investment programs are nondeferrable because they are so closely tied to regulatory compliance.

5. Harbridge House's use of a 35 percent dividend payout is unreasonably low in view of Ford's actual 39 percent average for 1967 to 1977 and its 44 percent average since going public in 1956. Using a 40 percent payout, Ford's cumulative maximum capital need under "normal" circumstances reaches almost $1 billion.

6. Harbridge House understates the difficulty of raising capital in a deep recession. Who would lend and purchase during such a period? What about the cost of capital? Could the company sell new common stock if it were

threatened with major dilution of its earnings, especially in light of the stock's current book value?

Ford seems to believe that the United States will experience a major recession in 1979-1980. A recession at that time would fall in the middle of Ford's major expenditure program and would directly affect its product planning for 1982 and 1983. This would be extremely costly to the company, especially since it seems very likely that Ford will be the UAW's target in 1982. This belief, along with its other assertions, makes it likely that Ford would propose some relaxation or stretching out by the rulemakers to ameliorate a recession situation if one should occur.

Essentially, Ford's ability to respond to even more stringent fuel economy standards post-1985 will depend on several factors—the reality of the $12.75 billion capital investment figure quoted by Ford for 1982 to 1985, the outcome of Ford's alternative-engine development program, the occurrence of a strike against Ford in 1982 (or in 1985), and the state of the U.S. economy through 1985. Ford could be in the best position of the Big Three to meet any post-1985 standards because of its package efficiency program and expected combustion technology advantage over the other companies. On the other hand, it could be in a critical financial position if many of its current programs and/or strengths fail. There are also some other factors that could make it difficult for the company to meet its obligations. These include the organizational risks involved in the succession changes scheduled to occur now through 1985, product liability exposure, the outcome of current litigation in which the company is involved, and, finally, the increasing threat that overseas governments will not allow the repatriation of offshore profits to the United States.

General Motors Corporation

General Motors believes that the impact of a two-year economic downturn would affect the United States more than West Germany or Japan, particularly with the continued deterioration of the dollar. To validate its argument, GM points to the 1974-1975 period, during which the domestic volume of cars produced by U.S. automakers dropped 22 percent below the average for the prior three years while the volume of cars sold in the United States by foreign manufacturers dropped only 2 percent. As a result, U.S. industry employment dropped 15.1 percent in 1975 (a loss of 181,200 jobs), and while U.S. industry sales revenues dropped only 6 percent, profits dropped 100 percent (to an aggregate loss in 1975).

Because the GM and Chrysler product mixes were tilted more toward large cars than the mixes of Ford or AMC, the impact of the energy-related downturn on these two companies was slightly greater than that experienced by either Ford or AMC. For example, GM's average unit volume in 1974 and 1975 was 23 percent lower than the average for the preceding three years, while Ford's unit volume dropped only 21 percent. Further, from 1973 to 1974 GM's sales revenues dropped 12 percent ($35.8 billion to $31.5 billion) and its profits dropped 60 percent ($2.4 billion to $1.0 billion) while Ford's sales during the same two years actually increased 3 percent, probably because of its greater relative involvement in overseas markets and its smaller car line, but profits dropped 45 percent.

General Motors is concerned about the effect that a recurrence of such a recession would have on its flow of funds. The company is traditionally dependent on the internal generation of funds to finance its next year's investment in new plants and tools and to pay for dividends. In 1974 its profits dropped $1.45 billion, and depreciation and amortization (major sources of funds at GM) dropped by $0.28 billion for a combined loss of $1.73 billion in internally generated capital. This shrinkage in cash flow had a significant impact on GM's disposition of capital. Broad actions taken by the company to compensate for this loss were (1) to initially allow the pool of working capital to reduce by $0.65 billion (previously working capital had tended to increase 5 percent to 10 percent each year); (2) to reduce dividend payments in 1974 by $0.58 billion and by $0.81 billion in 1975; (3) to increase long-term debt $0.24 billion in 1974 and $0.75 billion in 1975; and (4) to cease foreign investment, which saved about $0.1 billion in 1974 and a similar amount in 1975. Figure 1-1 shows the relationship between changes in GM's net income and depreciation and amortization (major sources of internal funds) and dividends and new investment in plant and tools (major uses of funds) from 1968 through 1977.

As can be seen from the figure, there tends to be a one-year lag in GM's reduction of purchases of new plant and tools after a drop in profits. Further, in the past reduced spending for plant and tools has tended to last two years, even though the loss of profits might only decline for one year, as in 1970, a strike year. It might be concluded from this that once GM deviates from its investment program, it takes two years for it to return to "normal" patterns of investment.

The slight downward fluctuation in depreciation in 1970 and 1974 is believed to be mostly the result of a volume-related reduction of tooling amortization. In 1974 the amortization expense of tooling dropped 20.6 percent over 1973, and the depreciation of the property, plant, and equipment dropped 6.2 percent.

General Motors has publicly stated that it will meet all CAFE/SDEN (corporate average fuel economy/safety, damageability, emissions, and noise) standards on time rather than absorb penalties for not meeting them. Because of its enormous financial strength and its relatively conservative position with respect to external financing, GM will have less difficulty than the other U.S. auto companies in meeting its investment requirements during a short (one- to two-year) downturn in volume of modest proportions. However, a recession of the magnitude of 1974-1975 would be difficult to deal with without retrenching on investment plans.

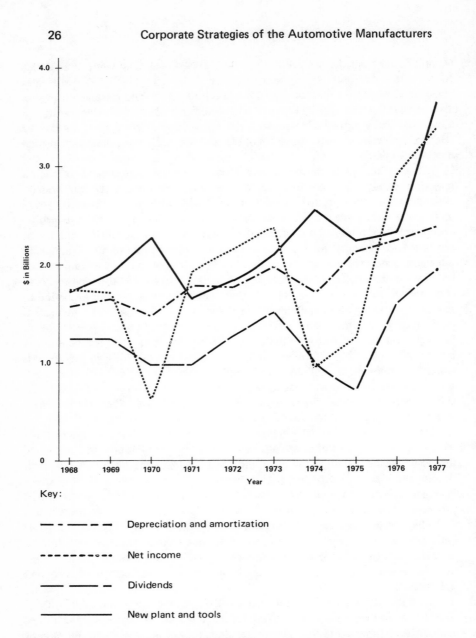

Key:

— · — · — · —   Depreciation and amortization

— — — — — ·· —   Net income

— — — — —   Dividends

——————   New plant and tools

Figure 1-1. General Motors' Major Internal Sources and Uses of Funds, 1968-1977

General Motors representatives have said that it would take a reduction of volume of about 10 percent or more below the average trend line to seriously affect its funds flow and concomitant disposition of capital. Projections made earlier in this section based on a 1974-1975 type of downturn (a 23 percent drop in GM's volume from the previous year) reveal that a two-year recession in, say, 1981 and 1982 would reduce available capital from internal sources by $5.64 billion (see table 1-5) from a "normal" projection (assuming an 8 percent per annum growth of revenue) of $10.5 billion in internally generated funds. The $10.5 billion is needed to meet GM's projected investment requirement of $10.9 billion for the same two years. Actually, this projected shortfall may be slightly understated because of the added effect of reduced depreciation and amortization at GM during a downturn. Based on the 1974-1975 experience, this might raise the capital deficit an additional 10 percent, from $5.64 billion to approximately $6.20 billion. In addition to this, it has already been estimated that GM would have to raise another $1.01 billion to cover the capital shortfall in "normal" years between 1978 and 1981.

Such a displacement of capital would seriously affect General Motors' ability to finance its investment needs. Most likely the company would try to raise large amounts of additional outside capital through long-term debt. General Motors has the debt capacity to do this, assuming that the capital is available in the enormous amounts needed. Moreover, even a drastic increase in GM's debt-equity ratio (from currently less than 10 percent to, say, 25 percent) would provide only $3 billion to $4 billion. The remainder of the deficit would have to be made up by a short-term reduction in working capital ($1 billion to $2 billion) and retrenchment on discretionary investment plans (for example, overseas expansion, styling changes, and other normal product modifications not related to CAFE/SDEN standards) by possibly as much as $1 billion to $2 billion. However, based on previous experience, this might not be realized until 1982.

The combined effect of such actions would yield some $4 billion to $6 billion in additional capital. Still, GM would probably experience a capital shortfall in 1981 that would require it to rely on even greater amounts of external funding (through more debt, taking it above a 25 percent debt-equity ratio, and/or new equity offerings). This would very likely not be acceptable to GM during a "normal" economy, much less during the negative economic conditions accompanying such a downturn (resulting in drastic increases in the cost and availability of external capital), even if the money were available, because of its impact on the financial structure of the company.

For example, in a recession scenario such as described above, the projected profits for GM at current levels of long-term debt would average $1.57 billion for the 1981-1982 period. If GM had to add $4 billion in long-term financing at a rate that might well exceed 12 percent during a 1981-1982 recession, the annual interest payments of $48 million would further reduce net profits by $0.24 billion (after taxes) to $1.33 billion. Such a level of profit would probably reduce dividends to 40 percent of their projected level for 1981-1982, making it harder to sell additional stock, and reduce return on equity to a level of approximately 6 percent (assuming a 10 percent per year growth in equity between 1977 and 1981). This would be a postwar record low for GM and completely mitigate its objective to raise its return on equity from previously dwindling levels.

Because GM has stated that it intends to meet the CAFE/SDEN standards on time, it might be concluded that the company does not anticipate a recession quite as severe as in 1974-1975. However, GM recently established some conservative financial strategies that seem to be intended to soften the impact of a possible recession. For example, GM is rumored to be attempting to lower the corporate break-even point—an action that companies usually take to reduce the sensitivity of profits to fluctuations in sales revenue. It has also tightened up on all spending at all levels in the corporation. Further, it would appear that GM is also attempting to pursue relatively less capital-intensive means of meeting CAFE/SDEN standards (for example, its current diesel program). These sorts of moves tend to reduce GM's exposure in a down market, which might indicate that the company expects a downturn in the not too distant future.

Although GM has not stated what its specific strategy would be if faced with a 1974-1975 type of recession, the company would very likely respond to such pressures in the following ways:

1. Try to persuade the EPA and NHTSA not to impose new emissions standards on diesels, which GM now sees as an important factor in meeting future fuel economy standards. General Motors projects that if new diesel emissions standards are not established, by 1985 some 25 percent of all U.S. new cars sold will be diesels.
2. Encourage the government to stretch out the time requirements on meeting fuel economy standards because of the shortage of capital needed to meet down-sizing programs. A likely approach would be to extend the 1985 deadline one year for each year that the recession lasts.
3. If necessary, also urge NHTSA to provide additional selective relief to the weaker members of the industry (that is, AMC and Chrysler) in order to ensure their survival.

Toyota Motor Company

Toyota's current product mix concentrates heavily on small cars with favorable fuel efficiencies. Its fleet average of cars exported to the U.S. market in 1977 was 28.5 miles per gallon, exceeding the mandated 1985 target of 27.5 miles per gallon. Its chance of meeting the 1985 standard is therefore quite good, even if some shift in the company's export product mix is considered. However, if a further tightening of the federal emissions control standards is proposed, this would inject an element of considerable uncertainty. In this case, again, Toyota would probably be able to manage the 27.5 miles per gallon requirement through perhaps a combination of adjusting its export product mix toward a higher proportion of smaller cars (which may necessitate some compromising of its optimal product strategy from a marketing viewpoint) and any fuel efficiency improvements achieved in terms of weight reduction and related effects.

Under a scenario of more stringent U.S. fuel economy standards in the post-1985 period (such as a fleet average requirement of 30 miles per gallon by 1990), Toyota's position can be summarized as follows:

1. By the 1990s the world's oil supply will not be sufficient to meet all gasoline requirements, and coal-derived gasoline will probably be used as a supplement. As a result, the quality of gasoline will be lower, which will also mean lower fuel efficiency for any given engine. Consequently, there is little reason to believe that there is any value in simply extending the current average miles-per-gallon figure, especially since there is a great deal of uncertainty as to what might be achievable technically.

2. Achievement of 27.5 miles per gallon (the 1985 goal) would drastically reduce the annual gasoline consumption of U.S.-made cars. Achieving this level with certainty is much more important than conjecturing about how much more mileage figures should be raised. But it is also much more difficult since it requires careful planning, not simply an extension of currently targeted figures.

3. At Toyota, if achievement of a fleet average figure of, for example, 30 miles per gallon by 1990 becomes a government requirement, this will basically entail refinements of the existing Otto-cycle engine technology from two directions, each of which contributes about equally to the process of reaching the results desired: reduction of car weight and improvements in efficiencies of the engine and different parts, particularly through reduction in friction-related losses. Viscosity of oil also plays a role here. Car weight is a big factor, especially at lower speeds. At low speeds 30 to 40 percent of potential overall improvements in fuel efficiency can be sought in weight reduction; air friction may contribute another 10 percent. At high speeds the relative significance of car weight is reduced while that of air friction increases. To deal with the air friction aspect, aerodynamic characteristics will be featured in styling—the new Celica design is a start in that direction.

Toyota's cars, particularly the larger models, contain substantial potential for weight reduction effects. For example, from the date of its introduction in 1968, to 1977, the Mark II (also called the Cressida) increased in weight as safety, comfort, and emissions control features were progressively incorporated into the vehicle and major and minor model changes were performed. In the 1977 remodeling of the car (1,800, 2,000, and 2,600 cubic centimeters) the weight was reduced 80 kilograms. As a result, the weight per square meter of projected area was reduced to less than 145 kilograms.

The kind of situation hypothetical for 1990—with the government fleet average fuel mileage requirement set at 30 miles per gallon—would no longer give Toyota an advantage over the U.S. auto manufacturers. In reaching the 1985 mileage requirement, Toyota is starting out with a relative advantage because of its past concentration on a small-car product mix. But by 1981 General Motors will have down-sized all of its product lines and will continue to make further improvements until 1985. As Toyota sees it, by 1985 it will be on a par with GM in terms of product-mix ability to meet upgraded fuel mileage requirements. Beyond 1985 searches for solutions will involve many new areas, and quite probably the transfer of satellite and aerospace industry technologies. Today Japan has no indigenous aerospace technology to speak of, and whatever it has is of little significance. This is one indication that beyond 1985 Toyota and the other Japanese automakers will have to extend more efforts than U.S. auto-makers to find breakthroughs to upgrade fuel efficiency. Further, these tasks will go beyond just meeting fuel mileage regulations to consider the entire quality aspect of automobile performance. Toyota thus anticipates some stiff technical competition, from GM and Ford in particular.

If a serious economic downturn comes either before or after 1985, Toyota's view is that any regulatory programs already in place and to which the automakers have made substantial resource commitments should not be changed, since either an upgrading or a downgrading of the regulations would represent additional costs. Given an assurance that regulations will be left unchanged, the automakers would try to manage the recessionary years as best they can while awaiting an economic upturn. In this process, however, some smaller automakers would find it impossible to continue operating, so that bankruptcy may result.

Nissan Motor Company

Nissan's position vis-à-vis the 1985 U.S. fuel economy requirements can be summarized as follows.

1. By assuming that the most strict nitrogen oxides emissions standards the United States will apply is 1.0 gram per mile, Nissan will be able to meet the 27.5 miles per gallon fleet average figure in 1985 with its current product mix. As long as U.S. consumers desire this mix, Nissan has no intention of changing it. The current average fuel economy of Nissan's exports to the U.S. market stands at 26.8 miles per gallon. To close the gap between now and 1985, Nissan will essentially concentrate its efforts on improving engine efficiency. To the extent that it is able to upgrade some of its product offerings the results of its engine efficiency improvement programs hold the real key.

2. If a U.S. nitrogen oxides regulation of 0.4 gram per mile is hypothesized, the task of meeting the 27.5 miles per gallon requirement in 1985 will be considerably more difficult. But, by adjusting its product mix downward to include a greater proportion of smaller cars, Nissan should be able to manage the fuel economy figure.

3. Car weight reduction will be involved to some extent, but a great deal has already been achieved in this regard, and the remaining potential is relatively limited. Plastics application will expand, but aluminum will not be too big a factor because of its high price in Japan.

4. As for the post-1985 period scenario of a possibly more strict fuel mileage regulation in the United States (for example, 30 miles per gallon in 1990), Nissan should theoretically be able to find a way to meet such a requirement. This will perhaps involve both concentrating the product mix on smaller cars (that is, those models with the 40-plus miles per gallon rating) to a considerable extent and mustering various technical improvements. How to fit such a product mix to market preferences could be a problem, however.

5. On the whole, Nissan feels that the Japanese automakers are in a better position than the U.S. automakers to meet any fuel efficiency requirements that the U.S. government may decide to mandate either before or after 1985. The Japanese cars are already small, and to the extent that Detroit could develop some technical approaches to meet the requirements with its larger cars, the Japanese automobile technology should also be progressing sufficiently to meet the same requirements.

There is a tendency developing that by the U.S. adoption of a 27.5 miles per gallon target figure for 1985, the Japanese automobile industry as a whole will be moving in a similar direction and, more or less, the auto industries in other countries as well. Regardless of whether the Japanese government eventually has an energy plan that includes a specific fuel mileage standard for the automobile, the Japanese auto industry will increasingly focus on fuel economy improvements. Even without U.S. fuel economy standards the industry's competition has come to concentrate on technical accomplishments relating to fuel efficiency characteristics. This tendency has strengthened lately, particularly since compliance with the series of passenger car emissions control standards has been completed in Japan. Of equal significance is the fact that Japanese consumers appreciate the merits of fuel efficiency when they purchase cars. Consequently, because the national objective of energy conservation has to a major degree become internalized in the Japanese marketplace, establishing a fuel mileage regulation in the country would very likely be unnecessary. The results of the industry competition to offer cars with good fuel efficiency characteristics should become increasingly evident in the Japanese market within two to three years as the fruits of current efforts are incorporated in the products.

Although Nissan does have the alternative of down-sizing its product mix by increasing the proportion of small fuel-miserly cars, its objective is to increase the fuel efficiency level of its cars by other means. This will basically involve a major emphasis on engine modifications and improvements. In order to improve engine efficiency characteristics, various R&D projects are currently being undertaken. Naturally, the results will not provide a perfect solution to simultaneously achieving a good fuel economy and eliminating pollutants emissions. Catalysts will continue to be needed, but through engine modifications and improvements fewer catalysts will be required.

Because considerable commitments are being made in comparable efforts by each of the Japanese automakers, a future economic recession could represent a serious financial problem, particularly for some of the smaller ones. A financially constraining effect could evidence itself if the currently depressed domestic market conditions which began in 1974 continue much longer.

Honda Motor Company

Honda achieved a fleet fuel economy of 33.7 miles per gallon on its 1978 models. With the product mix it is contemplating for the 1979-model year, and under the currently enforced emissions standards, Honda's fleet average will probably reach 35 miles per gallon. Given the new emissions standards—0.41 gram per mile for hydrocarbons, 3.4 grams per mile for carbon monoxide, and 1.0 gram per mile for nitrogen oxides—the company believes that a fleet average figure of 30 to 32 miles per gallon will be possible by 1985. To achieve this level of fuel economy, the company is carrying out various R&D programs to seek improvements in power train efficiency, car weight, aerodynamic styling, and refinements in the CVCC engine system.

Honda believes that "technology improves daily" and that from 1978 to 1985 fuel efficiency improvements of 3 to 5 percent are quite possible, especially if the U.S. emissions control standards now timetabled do not change. As a result, a hypothetical case of, for example, a U.S. fuel economy fleet average requirement of 30 miles per gallon in 1990 would appear to be within Honda's reach. If a higher fuel economy is hypothesized, it would probably involve shifting the company's sales mix to concentrate on the most fuel-efficient models. However, a standard like 40 miles per gallon in future years would be difficult to meet.

The R&D efforts related to power train efficiency, car weight reduction, aerodynamic design, and refinements of the CVCC engine system will require considerable financial commitments by Honda. Consequently, if there were to be a major recession lasting two to three years, Honda might encounter severe difficulties; but as long as the recession were of a more common cyclical variety, the company should remain viable while incurring these expenditures.

Honda, a small-scale automaker, offers the following points of view in assessing the various implications of the scenarios described:

1. Because it is a business enterprise that has shareholders, it would be criminal for the company to lose money.

2. Regulatory requirements add costs that have to be incorporated into the price of the product. These costs are basically the same for both large and small cars and large- and small-scale automakers. However, given two products of equal

quality, the one with a lower price will sell. Thus, the larger makers for whom the regulatory cost impact is relatively less have a greater profit margin and/or an option to offer a low price. Given the potential antitrust problem, the largest of the automakers would probably not fully exploit the opportunity to price its products in a low price range which makes such a price untenable for smaller makers to compete. Nonetheless, the inherent tendency under major regulatory programs which incur large sums of money is for the larger makers to increase their profits and/or expand their market shares. As this tendency increases and competitive pressures intensify as a result, it becomes less and less possible for the smaller automakers to pass all the costs related to regulatory programs on to the price of their products.

3. If more is left to the choice of the consumer and mechanisms of the marketplace rather than to government regulation, the potential for a smaller manufacturer to compete would be greater. This observation results from the fact that the market demand for a particular product is decided by both the absolute value of the product and its relative value vis-à-vis the products offered by the competition. This mechanism has the inherent tendency of causing the large makers to close in on the already small market shares held by the small makers; this is because the relative value of the small maker's product is largely defined by the broad market offerings and prices of the large maker(s). In this regard, as less is left to the consumer for making a value judgment on a product and more aspects of product characteristics are defined by the government, the opportunity and challenge for a small maker to offer a product with original and unique value qualities become more and more limited. Honda believes that, despite these growing constraints, its way will be to continue to pursue the development of products with unique features which respond to consumers' needs and which enhance the relative value of the products. By these means it hopes to be able to maintain or even expand its market share against those of the large makers.

Honda basically weighs the following factors in making product development decisions to accomplish this goal:

Price

Percentage of disposable income spent by the consumer

Life-style that determines a given utility concept of the automobile

Value perceived by the consumer regarding the various attributes of an automobile, including technical features, styling, interior design, performance and power, finish, and accessories

Consumer loan period

Economy of the automobile in terms of maintenance and fuel efficiency (the significance of this factor may not be too great, however)

Responsiveness to various social needs and the potential to create demand (Honda's CVCC engine met the emissions control requirement early. Honda was able to capitalize on this fact to build the reputation of the company and its products).

Profits

Volkswagen AG

If an economic recession comparable to that of 1974-1975 were to reoccur, the following would probably result: increased unemployment because of a significant drop in the gross national product; a decline in new-vehicle sales caused by a sharp decline in the demand for large vehicles so that smaller, lower-priced cars would become more attractive; the introduction of auto import restrictions.

In assessing the probable impact of these events on Volkswagen and how the company would react, certain facts should be considered:

1. VW sells 2.2-plus million vehicles in some 120 countries.
2. In 1977 approximately 15 percent of VW's total production was sold in the United States.
3. In the future VW will supply the U.S. market mainly from U.S.-based production facilities, but some of this U.S. production will eventually be exported to Canada.
4. The Volkswagen of America operation will have its own engineering and design functions (as does VW of Brazil), but engine and other developments that are expected to have the most significant fuel consumption impact will remain concentrated in Germany.

The U.S. automakers—primarily General Motors—have developed investment plans that are very dependent on financial results achieved. This cannot be said for VW. As table 1-6 shows, there appears to be no correlation between sales and profits (reserves are made and dissolved to produce an apparent equal earnings picture over the years); and investments are not directly related to earnings, sales, or depreciation.

Volkswagen will be able to meet the 1985 fuel economy standards without making any further investments. It will be able to achieve even more stringent fuel economy standards by:

Downsizing in conjunction with the use of lightweight-construction principles. Here VW claims to fully represent the current state of the art.

Improved engine efficiency. Here VW has already made, and is planning further, substantial investments to perfect its diesel engines by introducing onboard minicomputers for fuel injection and emissions control. These investments would probably not be directly affected by a 1974-1975 type of recession.

Improved tire designs (to reduce tire-road friction). Given the strong competition among tire manufacturers, further substantial improvements are expected in this area.

Since the oil crisis VW has emphasized small-sized economy cars in its product planning. It has also predicted a strong demand in low-horsepower versions of its small cars (for example, the Polo). However, with actual demand mainly for larger-sized models in larger-engine versions, VW has been able to switch its production to larger models and larger engine sizes. Similarly, VW is expected to be able to accommodate the changing demands of a serious recession by offering smaller engine versions for the Rabbit, Dasher, and Audi models and increasing its diesel penetration of total engine production.

In summary, VW is in a far better position than any U.S. manufacturer to meet current fuel efficiency standards. Its ongoing investments in further engine refinements will most probably enable the company to meet even more stringent standards after 1985. In the past VW's RD&E investments have not been influenced substantially by the company's financial results. Today it has the resources available to finance necessary investments, even if sales and earnings were to fall substantially during a recession period.

Volkswagen will most probably continue to invest substantially in new technologies if it anticipates sufficient market potential for that research, regardless of whether it faces a downturn in sales (as in 1972) or a recession and consequent loss situation (as in 1974). Even a substantial increase in earnings (as in 1973) would probably not influence its technological investments significantly since these are apparently planned on a long-term basis and are thus relatively "frozen."

Table 1-6
Volkswagen Group Results

	1971	1972	1973	1974
Sales (DM million)	17,310	15,996	16,982	16,966
Percentage change over previous year	–	(8)	6	none
Net Earnings (DM million)	147	206	330	(807)
Percentage over previous year	–	40	60	(245)
Depreciation (DM million)	912	1,237	1,221	1,260
As percentage of sales	5.2	7.7	7.2	7.4
As percentage of net earnings	620	600	370	–
Investments (DM million)	1,925	1,573	1,556	1,883

Notes

1. Ford announced worldwide spending of $30 billion, of which approximately 85 percent represents capitalized items.

2. Chrysler announced a U.S. capital investment of $3.75 billion for 1978 through 1982 plus an additional $1.0 billion overseas; analysts estimate additional capital investment of $1.5 billion for 1983 through 1985.

3. Assuming an annual rate of inflation of 5.5 percent to 1985, approximately one-third of the increments listed would be accounted for by future inflation while the balance would be investment in 1978 dollars.

4. *Normal*, as defined earlier, means an environment where Ford's revenues and profits increase 8 percent per annum, markets remain unchanged, no recession through 1985, and so forth.

2

The Impact of Product-Liability Trends on Automaker Ability to Comply with Existing Restraint Legislation

Harbridge House Overview

General

With the implementation of federal Motor Vehicle Safety Standard (MVSS) 208 currently mandated to be implemented in 1982, certain occupant safety measures will begin to be phased in. These include the installation of a passive-restraint system—passive belts and/or air bags—on standard-sized cars in the 1982-model year, on intermediates and compact cars in the 1983-model year, and on subcompacts and minicars in the 1984-model year. Both General Motors and Ford have already announced plans for offering passive restraints (belts or air bags) as options prior to 1982.

Because the standard is mandated and because all members of the industry intend to comply with it, there is no need to discuss the standard itself. However, in view of the fact that product liability is the fastest-growing area of negligence law, what does need to be evaluated is the direct impact of the automobile industry's compliance to this performance standard. There are essentially three sorts of issues to be addressed: questions concerning auto manufacturer safety design choices, uncertainties in the tort litigation system, and the ability of automobile industry manufacturers and suppliers to insure themselves against product-liability exposure. In addition, product liability needs to be looked at from the broader perspective of being a potential barrier to innovation in the auto industry. All these issues and the broader perspective are discussed in detail.

Automobile Manufacturer Safety Design Choices

There are three potential ways in which U.S. automakers could be legally liable relative to MVSS 208: by failing to install a passive-restraint system until mandated to do so when the technology has been available (at least since 1975); through failure of the air cushion restraint system (ACRS) to function as intended and the consequent recall exposure; and through a decision to use a passive belt system in lieu of an ACRS.

The first potentiality is one which may or may not be a serious threat to the industry. However, because there seems to be sufficient question surrounding this issue, it does require further study and analysis. Essentially, there are historical and legal precedents which, coupled with current court trends, could make it difficult for a court to decide in favor of the auto industry if such a lawsuit should develop. One such case, the *T.J. Hooper* case decided by Judge Learned Hand in 1932, involved the owners of a tugboat and barge that sank with cargo aboard. A suit brought against the barge owners by the cargo owners was decided in favor of the plaintiff on the grounds that the tugboat did not have a radio receiver, considered to be a reliable, reasonably priced, and readily available piece of equipment. Although radio receivers were not commonly found on tugboats in the 1930s, the judge ruled that the lack of such a receiver was evidence of negligence and, therefore, a direct contributor to the damage done to the cargo.

In a much more recent case (*Barker* v. *Lull Engineering Co.*, January 1978), the Supreme Court of California also decided in favor of the plaintiff, shifting the burden of proof onto the defendant. Its decision was based on the following ruling of strict liability:

> A product is defective in design if the plaintiff proves the product's design proximately caused injury and the defendant fails to prove, in light of relevant factors, that on balance, the benefits of the challenged design outweigh the risk of danger inherent in such design.

Accordingly, this decision could have some far-reaching impacts on the auto industry if it is not able to prove that the benefits of passenger cars without air bags (or other passive restraints) outweigh the risks inherent in offering them to the general public, at least as an optional piece of equipment.

This ruling was reversed by the *Daly* v. *General Motors* case in which the plaintiff was not awarded recovery of damages. Although it is still too early to tell what will be the net result of the contradictory outcomes of these two cases, Professor Richard A. Epstein of the University of Chicago Law School, one of the leading tort law professors, believes that the courts will continue the trend of awarding in favor of the plaintiff and impugning manufacturers for their past actions.

There have been many other cases in transportation history where manufacturers have resisted changing existing systems in order to incorporate safety devices. Probably the most classic one involved the Westinghouse automatic air brake. It took a full twenty-four years before this item was standard on all trains. In creating a rationale for its failure to comply, the railroad industry claimed that the cost and complexity of the intended device made its use prohibitive. The automobile industry is now using this very same argument. Yet, according to many automotive industry members and observers, the cost argument, when applied to air bags, is a highly questionable reason for not installing air bags or at least offering them as optional items. When the cost of other optional equipment items is compared to that of air bags, as is shown, it is difficult to argue in favor of the auto industry.

1976 Chevrolet Nova		1976 Ford Granada	
Air conditioning	$479	AM/FM radio with tape player	$299
Power windows	140	Power-operated sunroof	517
Air bag	233	Air bag	235[1]

Second, relative to the complexity of installing and operating a passive-restraint system, there are those who would quickly claim that "a certain degree of complexity in construction is sometimes necessary for simplicity in operation." Certainly, the auto industry, because of the technological innovations it has developed over the years, must be considered capable of solving the technological complications of such a system.

The third argument (one that is not applicable in all states[2]) is that the auto industry has elected to install active seat belts instead of air bags, even when air bag technology has been available for some time—yet some 70 to 80 percent of consumers do not use their seat belts. Because "driving without a seat belt is an entirely foreseeable use of the vehicle" (*Horn* v. *GM*, 1976) according to the California Supreme Court, and a District of Columbia court ruled that "to characterize plaintiff's behavior in this case as lacking in ordinary prudence would be paradoxical, as it did not differ from that of 75 percent of the motorists in this country with respect to the use of seat belts" (*McCord* v. *Green*, 1976), the choice of active seat belts is not one that the automakers could easily defend.

These decisions would likely raise the issue of whether a reasonable alternative were available to a manufacturer in selecting a safety device (such as the air bag) and, if so, whether strict liability were attached to failure by the manufacturer to select such an alternative.

It must be concluded from the above that there is a possibility of the auto manufacturers' being potentially liable for those years when air bags have been available for use (at least since 1975) and they have chosen not to use them.

The second potential problem related to manufacturer safety design choices involves the failure of the ACRS to function as intended; NHTSA estimates that 300,000 vehicles annually are involved in crashes in which an air bag should deploy. Even if 99.4 percent of all air bags are reliable, some 1,800 autos per year would be equipped with defective ones that would fail to deploy on impact. Moreover, although there is essentially no difference in a manufacturer's product-liability exposure, whether the matter at issue is the installment of a passive-restraint system or energy-absorbing bumpers, when air bags are the issue, the heightened expectations of the increasingly knowledgeable and powerful consumer as well as members of the legal profession who will try to take advantage of the situation, coupled with a nonuniform and rather uncertain tort litigation system nationwide, mean that total liability exposure (and consequent recall) can be quite extensive.

A third way in which automaker safety design choices increase product-liability exposure involves the choice of a passive belt system in lieu of an air bag. Certainly, it is to the manufacturer's advantage to use passive belts—less complicated technology, less costly components, and an inherently smaller liability exposure. Moreover, it will be very difficult to install air bag systems on the small cars of the future. However, given current trends, it is possible that a court would decide in the plaintiff's favor in a case where injury was received by the occupant of a vehicle that did not have an air bag system because the manufacturer chose, instead, to install a passive belt system, even though the occupant elected to disconnect the belt. This supposition is based on an issue which is not treated consistently in state tort law—whether the contributory negligence of the plaintiff (disconnecting a passive belt) can be introduced by the defendant (automaker) to reduce economic recovery for the plaintiff. Manufacturers can be sued under strict liability law based on product defect or under negligence law. Under strict liability some states allow comparative negligence (of both plaintiff and defendant) to be introduced, while other states do not consider plaintiff negligence at all. Under negligence law, contributory negligence on the part of the plaintiff is admissible in some states, whereas in other states only comparative negligence is allowed to be introduced. Needless to say, this inconsistency in state tort litigation systems creates more risk and uncertainty for today's manufacturers.

Uncertainties in the Tort
Litigation System

Actually, the tort litigation system itself has brought about much of the product-liability problem. Rules are constantly changing (and are then retro-actively applied) in each of fifty-two different jurisdictions (all federal courts and the District of Columbia), and, given that the product liability issue is likely to grow worse, these operational uncertainties are causing much concern. According to a recent Department of Commerce report, most of the recom-mended actions concerning product liability are for tort law reform.[3] They include:

> Modifying the statute of limitations in state tort law to clarify and make uniform the length of time a manufacturer is liable for a product.

> Creating a compliance with defense of safety standards in order to establish the relevance of the consumer's conduct (contributory negligence) with respect to tort awards (plaintiff's economic recovery).

Eliminating the awarding of punitive damages. Some states allow these; others do not. Some states include them as part of a general judgment; others do not; and so forth.

Professor Richard A. Epstein has used the crashworthiness-of-vehicles doctrine to highlight many of the problems created in the last ten years by the uncertainties of the current tort litigation system. It is his view that we cannot overestimate the seriousness of current court trends as they impact the auto manufacturers. One of the key trends seems to be a shift from use of the theory of negligence to that of strict liability. With this shift have come the following consequences:

1. The safety standard (for a product design) has become somewhat higher than it would otherwise be under a negligence standard, thereby demanding the best possible set of design choices.
2. The costs of discovering and implementing a new design technology must remain relevant under strict liability, short of holding an auto manufacturer responsible for all injuries to passengers no matter how they are caused.
3. It has enabled the California Supreme Court to circumvent traditional rules of evidence, such as the introduction of product improvement or modification by the manufacturer after an accident.
4. Defenses of abnormal use, assumption of risk, and contributory negligence, once available to defendants, have been severely cut back. Only plaintiff misuse which is completely unforeseeable constitutes a defense.
5. The affirmative defense based on the state of the art has been either restricted or eliminated, leaving the defendant with almost no defense.
6. The tenor of the times is in favor of the plaintiff's recovery with the burden of proof on the defendant.[4]

Some of the potential problems created by compliance with air bag legislation become readily evident by looking at GM's experience in offering the air bag on select new-car models in the 1976-model year. According to one U.S. government report,[5] the ratio of lawsuits to air bag deployments was so high that GM discontinued the option.

Another strong hint of the potential problems surrounding this issue was voiced by Eaton Corporation, the pioneer developer of the air bag project, which abruptly announced in December 1977 that it had decided not to manufacture air bag components. Along with questions regarding the market size and consequent return on its $20 million to $25 million investment, another key reason given by Eaton for dropping out of the air bag market was concern about the unresolved product-liability aspects of the air bag which, in its view, would necessitate federal product-liability indemnification to stimulate large-scale manufacture and use of the device.

Ability of Automobile Industry
Manufacturers and Suppliers to
Insure Themselves against
Product-Liability Exposure

According to the Final Report of the Interagency Task Force on Product Liability, completed in November 1977,

> There is no real problem of insurance availability except for a few companies in high-risk product lines; policy limitations that insurance companies are willing to underwrite for product coverage have not changed significantly since [The Task Force's Briefing Report, January] 1977. However, some underwriters are not willing to *increase* the limitation for manufacturers whose product risk exposure is increasing.

In addition, the study determined that comprehensive general liability coverage premiums (primary coverage including a deductible, plus umbrella or excess risk coverage) have increased nearly 207 percent from 1971 to 1976, and a total of 119 percent from 1974 to 1976. Moreover, total insurance costs for major companies (over $100 million in sales) have been in the range of 0.1 to 0.9 percent of total sales. These costs include premiums, uninsured costs of payments to others, and internal costs not covered by insurance. Premiums represent the largest cost increase, averaging a 200 percent increase from 1975 to 1976.

Internal costs for the automakers include a deductible, or self-insured retention (SIR), which is approximately $2.5 million per claim. Ford and Chrysler both have captive (in-house) companies to underwrite this insurance while GM uses a commercial insurer for its SIR and excess risk (totals of up to $10 million per claim). Considering that the compensatory damages in the recent *Grimshaw* v. *Ford Motor Co.* settlement involving a Pinto rear-end collision and subsequent gas tank explosion (February 1978) were $2.8 million and subsequently reduced to $2.6 million, the SIR would essentially cover it. However, the plaintiff was also awarded punitive damages of $125 million (subsequently reduced to $3.5 million) which were not covered. In another suit that was filed against GM in 1976 for $8.3 million by a Buick owner who alleged that his air bag did not inflate in a near-fatal collision,[6] it would seem that GM, too, would have sufficient coverage to insure against the compensatory damages. However, considering all potential damages, and from the insurance industry's point of view, the question to be asked is, What is the order of magnitude of the automakers' total exposure, especially when the issues dealt with above are taken into account?

Insurance companies deal with averages and predictability and are concerned about the severity and frequency of claims relating to them. The companies underwrite risk based on determination of total exposure, without any statutory limits attached to strict liability or any degree of certainty relative to the tort litigation issues already discussed. Thus, it is difficult for insurers to determine total auto manufacturer exposure (total product-liability exposure equals yearly unit sales volume times total time limit times average value) and to effectively insure the automobile industry against it. When the availability of alternatives and high inflation are factored into the equation, the predictability and uncertainty of product-liability exposure are compounded.

Although exposure predictability is uncertain, according to members of the insurance community, there does not seem to be any real question as to the availability of risk insurance for the auto industry in regard to passive-restraint systems. Because the casualty insurers anticipate fewer bodily injury claims and/or possibly smaller claims, they also anticipate an overall net advantage in such a system. Moreover, where potential problems exist because of tort law, counsel for the insurance industry is working to alleviate these for both the insurance and the manufacturing industries.

Broader Implications of Product-Liability Trends

In addition to the specific impact of product liability trends on compliance with passive-restraint legislation, there is a much broader implication insofar as it may be a barrier to future innovation in the auto industry. The risks stemming from the uncertainty of technical reliability, regulatory requirements associated with technological innovation, and the costs involved are all almost equally effective barriers to innovation according to a recent U.S. Department of Transportation-sponsored study.[7] In another study[8] it was concluded that where innovation is moving slowly, it is essentially due to market uncertainties, risk considerations, and irregularities in the decision-making behavior of the companies involved (based on their objectives, return-on-investment expectations, and so on).

Moreover, although the technical reliability of a product or component may ultimately be achieved, the cost of that achievement as well as the benefits to be derived by both the manufacturer and society at large must be determined. Are they worth the costs involved? Eaton Corporation is an excellent example of a company that had to deal with this cost/value determination issue, finally deciding that the cost-to-benefit ratio was not sufficient for it to continue to work toward manufacturing air bags. This experience also led to Eaton's decision to never again become involved in developing products that can be evaluated so subjectively and that are so emotionally charged.

Public Policy Options

In discussing the impact of product-liability trends on the automakers, and especially on their ability to comply with the 1982 safety standards, we have tried to surface some of the public policy issues that need to be addressed. These issues present some options which need to be considered in depth by the safety regulators:

Stretching out the period of implementation on the safety standards to achieve higher levels of system reliability

Following up Interagency Task Force options by the drafting of model product-liability legislation for states by the federal government and/or adopting a uniform federal product liability law

Creating some form of federally financed excess-risk insurance program

Scrapping the obligatory hardware approach to the problem and introducing a "software" approach in order to induce casualty insurers to offer customers low-cost bodily injury policies that pay off only if front-seat accident victims are wearing the current three-point seat belts

It is obvious that there are shortcomings in each option. However, the problems highlighted with respect to the current tort law and product-liability trends necessitate some concerted action by the federal government to more effectively respond to the needs of everyone concerned.

American Motors Corporation

American Motors Corporation is involved in safety research on a limited basis only. Despite recent federal regulations on occupant safety, its research and development expenditures have only increased from $35 million in 1974 to $43 million in 1977. Because a budget of this size does not allow for any basic research, AMC's efforts are confined to applications engineering, and most of this is done in conjunction with suppliers. Engineers at AMC usually provide the specifications, or sometimes they formulate a new idea and give it to a supplier who who will then develop the necessary hardware. The staff at AMC engineers the safety device into the car and supervises the testing, which is quite often contracted out to independent research institutes.

Increases in AMC's research activities are expected to be primarily in the vehicle testing area since new regulations can no longer be met by simply adding equipment, but instead require an integrated approach toward the vehicle as a whole. To date, current safety regulations have increased AMC's dependence on GM for expertise and components. This trend is expected to continue as new regulations are imposed.

American Motors Corporation has two primary concerns regarding product liability: the effect that the introduction of passive-restraint systems may have on the number of liability suits brought against the company and rapidly rising insurance costs.

So far AMC has had only a few liability suits brought against it, and most of these have not been related to safety. Moreover, no punitive damages have been awarded against the company. However, because of GM's brief experience with air bags, AMC expects a rapidly increasing number of liability suits once these become standard equipment; AMC sees this problem as being compounded by the lack of uniformity and explicitness in state and federal legislation concerning limits of liability settlements. It is very much aware of the fact that if a few large liability claims were to be brought against the company, these could have a disastrous effect on its profitability.

In the case of air bags, AMC believes that the liability problem could be alleviated if the lead time for incorporating air bag systems into passenger cars is stretched out and if explicit liability limits are established for the auto manufacturers. According to an AMC spokesperson, an air bag system can be disconnected just as easily as a passive seat belt; thus, choosing a passive seat belt system over an air bag would not increase the company's liability risk in a situation where a passenger disconnected the system.

Despite the small number of liability suits brought against AMC, its insurance costs have risen rapidly in the past few years, and its insurance costs per car have practically doubled within two years. Although the total costs are still relatively small, if the trend should continue, it will be only a few years before insurance costs begin to have a noticeable impact on AMC's profitability. Because of the company's financial condition, it cannot afford large deductibles. Consequently, its liability insurance coverage includes a deductible of only $0.5 million per claim. To limit its insurance premiums, the company has agreed to a maximum coverage of $35 million per year. Accordingly, AMC is very interested in the establishment of explicit liability limits.

Until recently AMC's recall record was the best in the industry. Because of its heavy reliance on component suppliers, however, the company's exposure to the risk of recalls is greater than that of the other U.S. automakers. To counter this risk, AMC instituted a program to improve quality control as soon as recalls became an issue. This program was facilitated by the high degree of concentration of AMC's manufacturing facilities.

American Motors Corporation believes that as the number of government standards and regulations increases, it is almost inevitable that the number of violations and recalls will also increase. So far the major problem caused by product recalls has been a tarnishing of AMC's image, especially when compared with the imports which, despite their poorer recall record, seem to receive far less adverse publicity than the domestic producers. In recent years AMC has set aside increasing reserves to pay for recalls, but so far these have not had a noticeable impact on the company's profitability.

Chrysler Corporation

Chrysler has had its share of recall campaigns and liability suits. Within one six-month period alone the company had to mount four recalls of its Aspen/Volare line, some of the recalls involving up to 1.2 million vehicles. In fact, when the last recall, involving a potential front-end suspension defect, was announced in May 1978, the company was still processing its previous two recalls which involved faulty hood latches and an engine stalling problem. Moreover, the company's new subcompact Omni/Horizon models had to be checked for a potential safety defect when they were still on the dealer lots; then, three months after their introduction, the entire production had to be recalled for a suspension problem. With an unfavorable article published in the July 1978 issue of *Consumer Reports*, a Consumers Union publication, which criticized the characteristics of these new models, Chrysler feared that the whole production of its minicars would have to be recalled again. A subsequent report by NHTSA refuting the Consumers Union's criticism averted this possibility. It also seems to have curbed the effects of the bad publicity generated so that the success of these new models has not been thwarted.

Chrysler has suffered setbacks in liability suits as well. One such suit, filed in Wisconsin in 1972, involved a woman who had become comatose after the 1964 Plymouth in which she was riding, driven by her husband, collided with an oncoming car that tried to make a left turn in front of them. This suit was brought by the injured woman's family against the driver of the oncoming car as well as against her husband on the basis that both individuals were driving in a negligent way, and against Chrysler because the coma was allegedly caused by the woman's hitting her head against a defectively designed rear-view mirror. (In 1967 new safety standards ruled out the use of this kind of mirror.) The husband of the victim and the driver of the oncoming car each had insurance coverage for $15,000, which was grossly insufficient to provide for treatment of the victim. Accordingly, the jury decided that the driver of the oncoming car was negligent for 10 percent, that the husband was not negligent in any way, that the woman was negligent for 1 percent because she was not wearing a seat belt at the time of the accident, and that Chrysler was negligent for the remaining portion. As a result, Chrysler had to pay approximately $1.5 million in damages.

Despite the trend toward more recalls and the willingness of courts to accept a broader interpretation of the notion of liability, the general feeling at Chrysler is that these trends have not yet reached a magnitude where they would have a sizable impact on the company's operations. No doubt recall campaigns are very costly but, despite the high incidence of recalls in 1977, Chrysler's total recall expense that year was still only a fraction of its warranty expense. When recalls succeed one another within a short period, the company can limit its expenses by checking the recalled cars for several defects at the same time.

If the number of recalls increases in the next few years at the same rate as in the last two, recall expenses will represent a heavy burden on Chrysler's profit margin. However, Chrysler is confident that the sudden increase in recalls in the last year is an exceptional situation that will not repeat itself. Actually, until 1977 Chrysler's recall record was the second best in the industry after AMC's.

Apart from the cost issue, recall campaigns and the accompanying bad publicity may have a negative impact on Chrysler's image. The company feels, however, that this problem will become serious only if it affects its competitive position, and that as long as all manufacturers are hit by recalls, they will all get their share of bad publicity. Consequently, the competitive situation has remained unchanged.

The product-liability issue has not yet become a major problem, but the numerous uncertainties surrounding it—for example, what standard of design a manufacturer can be held to, the extent of damages that may have to be paid, and the lack of coordination between federal and state legislations—cause concern about the future.

It is not yet clear what affect the introduction of passive-restraint systems may have on Chrysler's liability situation. It is indicative of this uncertainty that Allstate Insurance Company, for example, has not yet committed itself to an estimate of the insurance cost of any additional product-liability coverage. However, Chrysler is confident that it does not expose itself to a difference in risk simply by opting for one restraint system in favor of another.

Chrysler is currently involved in approximately 900 liability cases (the number of such cases has not increased substantially in the past few years). However, its insurance costs are increasing rapidly, and its total liability costs, including insurance premiums, have almost doubled within the last two years. Even though on a per-car basis these costs are still a small fraction of the company's unit profit margin, the trend is worrisome. Chrysler is insured by commercial insurers for claims exceeding $2 million. As insurance premiums continue to rise, the company is expected to increase this self-insured retention of $2 million per claim as one means of alleviating the high costs of insurance.

As in the case of recalls, Chrysler feels that as long as product liability does not affect the company's competitive position, it is not a strategic issue.

Ford Motor Company

Ford Motor Company's exposure to product liability has dramatically increased since 1972, especially in the last year as the company's involvement in major liability lawsuits has increased (such as in the *Grimshaw* v. *Ford Motor Co.* case whereby compensatory and punitive damages awarded to the plaintiff were initially set at $128 million and then reduced to $6.1 million) and as the number of government recalls initiated by NHTSA, the EPA, and the Federal Trade

Commission (FTC) has soared. In fact, Ford has been involved in more recalls than any other U.S.-based auto company. Moreover, the national media coverage of the *Grimshaw* case and of several other Pinto accidents has heightened consumer awareness of Ford's situation and has probably also served to increase the likelihood that more accident victims will seek compensation in the future.

Motivated by NHTSA, Ford issued a statement to recall its 1971- to 1976-model year Pintos (1.5 million cars). Previously, the company had been caught in a bind because it was actively involved in litigation of the *Grimshaw* case and thus was not able to comment on allegations concerning the Pinto's problems. Ford's continuing silence on the subject undermined consumer confidence in its products. It probably also did more damage to the Ford image than if the company had admitted its mistake, taken the consequences, and recalled all Pintos on its own initiative. In fact, the Pinto situation has been particularly significant for Ford, not only because of decreased Pinto sales but also because of the consumer disaffection that resulted, a disaffection that has already outlived Ford's actions to solve the Pinto's problems and may even have contributed to the risk of decreased sales of its new, higher-margined, upscaled Ford Division full-sized cars. Ford also fears the loss of public confidence and the erosion of its brand-loyal customer base.

In 1977 alone Ford recalled approximately 3 million vehicles produced in North America, representing 68 percent of its North American factory vehicle sales and 20 percent of all vehicles recalled by NHTSA in that year. (However, it should be pointed out that the company initiated 81 percent of these recall programs.) Because of a transmission problem the company is now faced with the possibility of the largest government-mandated recall of any auto manufacturer, involving 9 million cars manufactured between 1973 and 1978. The costs involved in such recall campaigns can be quite significant; the recall mail notices alone cost $1.00 to $1.50 per car.

A new liability dimension has been added by the FTC's intervention in situations relating to product performance. This intervention is beginning to mushroom, and Ford sees it as accelerating the already escalating product-liability exposure situation. The widely reported Ford "piston scuffing" case is one example of such a performance recall that has sensitized the company to its potential vulnerability.

Ford's major opportunity/risk relative to the product-liability issue concerns its ability to convince consumers that it is indeed being responsive to them. Realizing the importance of doing this, Ford has taken several initiatives in this direction: (1) it has organized a consumer board in North Carolina, a concept that is being expanded to several other states; (2) it has initiated a more active product quality-control program with more extensive damageability testing than ever before and has created a damageability standard for every car, all these being consistent with those of its competitors; (3) it has initiated its own recall campaigns; and (4) it has established a "hot line" for customers to use to report on automatic-transmission problems. Moreover, it has indemnified its dealers (through American Road Insurance Company, Ford's captive insurance company) for $5 million per claim.

As for punitive damages and insurance risks, Ford believes that its risk insurance *does* cover punitive damages, and the company has, in fact, brought suit against its fifty excess-risk insurers claiming such.

In light of its sensitivity to product-liability exposure in general, Ford's position relative to passive restraints is that these systems could cause some additional liability problems for the company, but not necessarily any greater than those it currently faces. These might be liability for occupant body injury at vehicle speeds lower than those required for air bag deployment (30 miles per hour), too high consumer performance expectations, and relative ease or difficulty in disconnecting passive belts.

General Motors Corporation

The current trends of an increasing number and greater frequency of product-liability suits, larger awards, more "liberal" interpretations of liability, and more aggressive NHTSA stances on recalls are of concern to GM, not only because of the growing costs related to liability insurance, settlements, and recalls, but also because of the amount of effort and attention these trends are diverting from innovative research programs to what might be termed *defensive* programs. Understandably, GM hesitates to put a price tag on the additional "costs" involved because such figures are hard to determine and can often be misleading. All GM will say is that the cost impact is "substantial."

Defensive measures taken by GM over the past several years include:

Increasing product engineering time and effort spent significantly in order to reduce potential defects. In 1977 GM had to recall 3,147,326 vehicles as a result of NHTSA actions. For the U.S. industry overall, 10.4 million vehicles were recalled while only 9.3 million new vehicles were sold that year. This was a 350 percent increase in recalls over the previous year. Naturally, GM would like to minimize the number of future recalls.

Increasing the standardization of components in order to keep costs down and increase productivity. Moreover, GM's product engineers and planners are even more inclined to keep reusing old, successful designs and to limit innovations unless these are absolutely necessary.

Establishing a program to indemnify its 13,700 dealers against liability claims emanating from retailing GM products. The GM plan adds a supplementary indemnification clause to the existing Sales and Service Agreement now in effect between each dealer and the GM car and/or truck division involved. The clause indemnifies dealers against lawsuits based on an alleged defect in the design, manufacture, or assembly of the product; claims that the product fails to conform to GM's advertisements or product brochures; damage repaired by the division prior to the time the product is delivered to the dealer. The dealer, in turn, agrees to indemnify GM against lawsuits based on dealer failure to properly repair a vehicle, dealer breach of contract with the customer, and false or misleading statements made by the dealer or its employees.

Establishing in 1977 a 300-person consumer services staff headed by James Vorhes. This group was formed to generally improve consumer and dealer relations, and apparently to reduce the number of potential consumer complaints and other problems.

Simplifying the language of warranties and extending them from ninety days to twelve months for certain parts.

Establishing training centers for automobile mechanics at no cost to dealers or trainees in an effort to improve the quality and effectiveness of GM authorized dealer service.

Establishing a dealer hot line with a central computer so that dealers can quickly determine by vehicle identification number whether outstanding recall work is required.

Establishing a program to reimburse dealers for warranty and recall work at the same labor rate they normally charge for nonwarranty work. This program is intended to give dealers an incentive to make an extra effort on warranty and recall work.

General Motors' position on MVSS 208 is that it will meet the standard on time. Until recently it appeared that GM would use the so-called passive seat belt approach rather than air bags. After having participated in early programs to develop air bags and becoming the only manufacturer to offer them as optional equipment in 1976 and 1977, GM appeared to be intent on abandoning them for a time for reasons of reliability, effectiveness, cost, and lack of market receptiveness. (General Motors cites only about 10,000 sales of air bags in three years, although many observers believe, and President Edward Cole agreed in 1974, that GM did not aggressively market air bags to its customers.) However, recent GM consumer studies show a consumer preference for air cushion restraint systems rather than passive seat belts. As a result, in the future GM may place more emphasis on the ACRS.

Whether trends in product liability have significantly affected GM's decision on air bags, or passive restraints overall, is not known. However, the GM engineering staff representatives interviewed about the effect of these trends on the product development process indicated that the impact was mostly on stretching out testing procedures and costs. We were told that "there currently does not seem to be any evidence that GM has become more cautious with regard to new and innovative products because of trends in liability." No figures were available at GM on the cost of recalls or liability claims.

Toyota Motor Company

Toyota's current position on product liability and U.S. occupant safety regulations can be summarized as follows:

1. Current developments in product liability and occupant safety regulations in the United States are in a major conflict as trends toward exaggerated treatment of product liability continue to grow. Excessive increases in both the number and the type of product-liability suits and the unpredictably large settlements involved are making every automaker who markets in the United States extremely cautious about introducing new products to the marketplace.

2. A complete reliance on hardware regulations to address automobile safety problems does not represent an optimal approach. Drivers and pedestrians are another important element in automobile traffic safety. Therefore, ways of improving their ability to reduce the risk of accidents must also be pursued.

Toyota does not want to deploy a technology in which it does not feel sufficiently confident technically. The company has been undertaking the development of air bag technologies, but the results to date have not been satisfactory. It acknowledges the possibility of reduced sales of Toyota cars since the uniform cost of air bags implies a larger cost increase relative to the price of a small car (like the ones that Toyota manufactures) than to the price of a larger, higher-priced car, so that market preferences may shift toward larger models. However, at present Toyota's primary concern is technical—if it solves its technical problems, it will adopt the air bag; if not, it will not use the device. The results of Toyota's own experiments show that active three-point seat belts are highly effective. Therefore, in terms of passive-restraint systems its preference and intent are to use passive seat belts because of the company's greater confidence in these in terms of technical reliability.

In its research on air bag technologies Toyota is giving special emphasis to sensor devices. This is because the small size of Toyota cars requires immediate activation of the air bag after a collision if that device is to be effective. Although it is testing radar sensors and G sensors, Toyota is not yet totally satisfied with either.

In summary, then, three factors are the basis of Toyota's current position vis-à-vis air bags: technical reliability; cost, in terms of unit cost and number of units applied (the company's current estimate of the increase in price for an air-bag-installed Toyota car is substantially higher than estimates prepared by either the U.S. Department of Transportation or the U.S. automakers); and usefulness of the devices. On all three counts Toyota is negative. However, if the use of air bags is mandated, Toyota's only recourse will be to try to develop the necessary technology in order to comply.

Nissan Motor Company

Nissan's view of traffic safety issues parallels those of the Japanese government and the Japanese automobile industry in general. By far the most pertinent issue is that of pedestrian safety because of the country's many narrow streets, despite the low speeds at which vehicles are driven through them. Road improvements and the use of both guardrails for segregating vehicle traffic from pedestrians and pedestrian overpasses have made considerable contributions to lowering pedestrian-related traffic accidents and, thereby, the nation's motor traffic-related death rate.

Vehicle occupant safety is not a big issue in Japan. Nonetheless, headrests were used in Japanese automobiles earlier than in U.S. vehicles. The possibility that air bags will become a prominent issue in Japan is rather small; the more likely alternative is increased use of active seat belts. Nissan's efforts, therefore, are continuing in terms of making seat belts more effective and more easily applicable than the ones currently in use. The company believes that the social and cultural environment of Japan makes it more conducive to get the public to use seat belts than would be the case in the United States.

Nissan's views on passive-restraint systems can be summarized as follows:

1. Passive-restraint systems should not be regulated, but if regulations are necessary, passive seat belts rather than air bags are preferred. The company's negative perception of air bags stems from the difficulty of ensuring their complete reliability since, even with the use of more sophisticated electronic devices, 100 percent reliability is difficult to obtain. Further, in order to protect occupants against lateral collisions, lap belts must be used in combination with air bags. The problem of whether to mandate the wearing of a lap belt and how to get the public to use it is the same as that pertaining to the existing three-point active seat belt, to which the air bag/lap belt combination is an alternative.

2. The inherent difficulty of ensuring 100 percent reliability points to product liability, and the current trend in product liability is toward increasingly liberal judgments against the manufacturer. Nissan has no way of estimating the

magnitude of product-liability implications from air bags. The problem is not as severe in Japan as in the United States at this moment, but the general direction is the same and the role of consumerism is growing.

3. A government regulation that stipulates the adoption of passive-restraint systems in the form of an either/or choice (the air bag or the passive seat belt) creates another uncertainty. Although Nissan prefers the passive seat belt, it is not able to determine which consumers prefer—air bags are more costly but less cumbersome than passive belts. Nissan is currently pursuing both courses and plans to install air bags on a limited number of cars.

4. Nissan is looking at all possible types of passive seat belt developments, including the Volkswagen system, but so far has not narrowed its choice to any one type. For example, the VW type requires a certain kind of door sash that would make it difficult to apply on Nissan's hardtop models.

Nissan has thus far obtained favorable results in its attempts to install and test the working of an air bag on its small-sized experimental safety vehicle (ESV). Research to determine how these results can be translated to application on mass-marketed Nissan automobiles[9] and how to heighten the reliability of air bags through better electronic mechanisms continues.

The company also finds it significant that some of the major U.S. manufacturers who were recently pursuing air bag development have decided to stop their activities in this area. The reasons for this given to Nissan were that U.S. automakers would not adopt air bags and U.S. regulations for these safety devices are likely to change again.

Honda Motor Company

In order to comply with U.S. passive-restraint system requirements, Honda is currently undertaking various R&D programs. Its position on both U.S. product-liability and occupant safety regulations can be summarized as follows.

1. The company has been carrying out an independent air bag R&D program. Based on the results to date, Honda's tentative conclusion is that it will likely be able to respond to MVSS 208. Because there are still some problems in applying its air bag technology to the company's mass-marketed cars (the fact that Honda cars are small poses some unique problems), it will continue its efforts to meet the deadline specified in the standard. To do this, it will probably need to use a phased approach.

2. Nonetheless, Honda has considerable reservations regarding the requirement for air bags since, first, there is no way to guarantee that all air bags will function correctly. To guarantee this means testing all air bags by inflating them; but once inflated, they are spent. Second, it is not possible to ascertain the continued effectiveness of an installed air bag throughout the life of a car. Third,

the air bag mechanism is so complex that there is no way at present to ensure that it will not inflate prematurely.

3. These issues related to reliability also have a nontechnical dimension—the potential for large product-liability disputes. The current trend suggests a growing gravity and scope in pressing a manufacturer's liability. Honda has no way of projecting the magnitude of the financial impact that might result from potential product-liability problems associated with a passive-restraint system regulation.

4. Honda also believes that the current state of the art in air bag technology and the regulation that relies on this technology have not progressed to the point of providing guaranteed protection in all types of collision, that is, diagonal, head-on, side, roll-over, and so forth.

Honda is therefore continuing its efforts to deal with these problems which are all part of the reliability question. The company will do its best to obtain a higher degree of product reliability by pursuing perfection of different sub-systems involved in air bag technology. It notes with considerable interest and concern the fact that the major U.S. auto components makers—who have had greater experience than Honda in this technology—have recently pulled out of the air bag business despite the considerable financial and workforce expenditures already invested in this venture.

In parallel to its experiments with air bags Honda is undertaking a program on passive seat belts, given that MVSS 208 allows automakers to choose between air bags and passive seat belts. Honda believes that the same type of product-liability questions implicating the air bag are also present in the passive seat belt, although not to the same extent. To Honda the fundamental issue, then, is which of the two passive-restraint systems the consumer will accept. Honda is also concerned that all these diverse efforts—parallel programs and continuous efforts to improve the reliability of either the air bag or the passive seat belt—plus liability insurance costs will eventually be so expensive that the consumer will have to absorb a large part of the cost. For example, Honda has been studying the side-collision problem and believes that it has found some solutions; these, however, will probably require increases in both vehicle cost and vehicle weight as well as reductions in fuel efficiency, interior space, and comfort. Even though it is difficult to ascertain the probable cost of the liability insurance, if the price of the automobile increases appreciably because of these potential cost-increasing factors, the consumer may begin to question the value of what the passive-restraint system requirement intends to accomplish.

Honda is pursuing the task of installing passive-restraint systems to comply with MVSS 208 with considerable reluctance. Fundamentally, it believes that the role of every automaker—by making decisions as to what represents a balanced product in terms of economics and product features—is to provide choices to the consumer who makes the ultimate choice. Moreover, Honda strongly believes that government vehicle safety programs that stress hardware requirements to the exclusion of other approaches are greatly amiss. Rather, it believes that to prevent accidents and to protect the safety of vehicle occupants, three important elements are required:

1. A vehicle's capability to avoid accidents.
2. Occupant protection once a collison has occurred—crashworthiness and design features/devices to minimize the impact as well as occupant injuries.
3. Software aspects relating to the interface between the driver and the vehicle—the driver's conscious actions (as external objects are perceived and commands are transmitted to the vehicle)—produce the vehicle's particular mode of movement and behavior. "Stationary cars do not cause accidents."

Even though certain safety aspects of the driver-vehicle interface process involve hardware (such as the weight of the steering wheel), Honda belives that there are many software-related improvements that government regulators should use to address safety features. For example, it believes that driver interest in and responsibility for avoiding inflicting injuries can and should be made part of the process of the conscious action of the driver in handling an automobile. Honda's objection to MVSS 208 is based more on the standard's one-sided emphasis on hardware at the neglect of important software potentials than on its related costs. In addition, Honda is uneasy about the technical reliability of passive-restraint systems and believes that attention should also be paid to the utilization of active systems.

Within Japan there is concern that implementation of MVSS 208 by the United States will increase pressure for adopting a similar requirement. However, it is Honda's opinion that philosophically Japan may be more socially amenable than the United States to address the subject of vehicle occupant protection in terms of individual driver responsibility. Nonetheless, the company is aware that heightened campaigns nationwide to educate the car-driving public about the merits of buckling active seat belts will, in itself, not solve everything. For example, a seat belt usage rate of 25 percent has been found only occasionally on certain expressways; moreover, according to research done by a seat belt manufacturer, the maximum seat belt usage rate that can be expected is 50 percent.

Volkswagen AG

It is assumed by Volkswagen that both the U.S. courts and the administration will act to increase consumer protection over the next few years. This implies a shift in emphasis in some states from strict liability to absolute liability and an increasing number of recall campaigns (both imposed and voluntary) with a considerable increase in the associated costs.

Most of the product-liability claims brought against VW relate to vehicle design defects, not production negligence. As a manufacturer-assembler, VW tries to pass these charges on to its components' suppliers. However, because of the increasing interdependency between the various components in a modern automobile, in the vast majority of cases VW is not able to prove that a specific component is defective. Thus, VW is only able to pass on about 1 percent of the total value of the claims brought against it to its suppliers.

Volkswagen claims that it wins the vast majority of product-liability cases brought against it (approximately 90 percent). The costs of these lawsuits are considerable. Although no detailed cost data were supplied (for reasons explained below), a rough estimate of the original cost of legal defense in product-liability lawsuits extending over several weeks was quoted as ". . . some $100,000." The size of the settlements in these disputes is viewed by VW as the cause of the increasing number of frivolous liability claims being made. ("We can too easily be 'blackmailed.' ") As for the costs incurred, VW feels that they will ultimately be passed on to the consumer through price increases all the way down the line.

In 1969 VW set up a corporate legal staff in Wolfsburg that, in coordination with its U.S. attorneys, handles all product-liability claims. A Volkswagen of America (VWoA) specialist only acts as a coordinator for Wolfsburg. Most actual decisions concerning claims settlements or recall campaigns are made in Wolfsburg by the corporate staff, which also advises VWoA on all product-liability decisions.

Like other auto manufacturers, VW treats all information relating to product liability as "corporate top secret." It is not willing to pass on critical cost and technical data because it fears that by opening its files to the public this information will become easily accessible to both its competitors and lawyers. Thus, it expects to go even further in "closing its doors."

Because the inspection and testing of purchased materials and components as well as quality control during and after production are expected to acquire even further importance at VW, the company will probably concentrate on fewer, larger suppliers, making it difficult for a new supplier to get approved (the engineers and purchasing officers are reluctant to take on an "unpredictable risk"). Further, VW's decreasing propensity to substitute components and materials will probably lead to the company's eventually working with fewer suppliers and thus negatively impact small- and medium-sized business.

In the future it is likely that VW will produce only very large volumes of fewer models and, to these, will apply rigorous quality assurance techniques. By producing such large volumes the company will be able to allocate the considerable costs of individual liability suits. For these reasons it is also likely that VW will direct its efforts to prolonging the economic life cycle of its existing high-quality cars and will introduce new cars only after extensive testing—even more than has been customary to date.

Volkswagen expects small business to feel the greatest negative effects of strict and absolute liability, claiming that today product liability is to a large extent already becoming uninsurable, and that as insurance premiums increase, small businesses are simply going to give up. Average product-liability insurance premiums are slightly less than 1 percent of revenues[10]—and VW claims it pays somewhat below this average. But for a company like VW with a return of sales of only 1.7 percent in 1977, increasing insurance premiums are sure to impact profits significantly.

Volkswagen believes that the U.S. trend of increasing liability is largely responsible for the slowdown in product improvements in recent years. Because strict liability in theory extends backward indefinitely, today's auto safety standards (state of the art) are used to assess the safety of vehicles produced some ten to fifteen years ago. Moreover, engineers are being asked to design cars today for unknown safety standards that may be enforced some five to ten years from now.

Notes

1. Versus the U.S. Department of Transportation estimate of $124.

2. In New York, for example, driving without the use of seat belts is considered to be evidence of contributory negligence. With this evidence, recovery damages would be reduced to the extent that a seat belt would have prevented injury.

3. *Final Report, Interagency Task Force on Product Liability*, U.S. Department of Commerce, November 1977.

4. Based on a statement by Richard A. Epstein, Professor of Law, to Joint Committee on Tort Liability of California Legislature on behalf of American Insurance Association, San Diego, July 18, 1977.

5. David Rothberg, "The U.S. Government Auto Safety Program; A Preliminary Examination," Massachusetts Institute of Technology Energy Lab Working Paper, December 1976.

6. Ibid.

7. Albert H. Rubenstein and John E. Ettlie, "Federal Stimuli to Development of New Technology by Suppliers to Automobile Manufacturers," March 1978.

8. Arthur D. Little, Inc., "Barriers to Innovation in Industry: Opportunities for Public Policy Changes," Report to National Science Foundation, September 1973.

9. Nissan believes that there is a major distinction between obtaining favorable test results in the limited and unique circumstance of a program such as the ESV project and implementing the same on mass-produced automobiles. Because of the obvious tendency of regulators to seize upon favorable experi-

mental results and to insist that manufacturers apply the experiments to a mass commercial application, the company is somewhat wary of being totally open about sharing information relating to its experimental programs.

10. *Final Report, Interagency Task Force on Product Liability.*

3 Emissions Control Standards and the Impact of Platinum-Group Metals Supply

General

Passage of the Clean Air Act of 1970 and its subsequent amendments have created the need for technological innovation in pollution control and have presented the automotive industry with its greatest challenge to date: to direct its efforts to simultaneously meet future mandated emissions control and fuel economy standards.

With the enforcement of tighter emissions control standards, catalytic converters, representing a new generation of pollution controls that no longer significantly reduce fuel economy and driveability, began to be installed on most U.S.-made cars in 1975. With this innovation, however, the auto industry has come face to face with a whole new set of problems. The first of them relate to ensuring a continued, uninterrupted supply of platinum-group metals (PGMs), the catalytic agents needed in the conversion process to eliminate toxic substances from automobile exhaust gas. Second, more stringent emissions control standards requiring the use of rhodium are to become effective in 1981. For the automotive industry this represents a unique technological problem as well as a potential but significant risk since the current platinum-to-rhodium proportion required in three-way catalytic converters (TWCs) is not the same as that found in the mined ratio, and therefore may result in a rhodium supply problem. Finally, because the U.S. Environmental Protection Agency may restrict the use of diesel engines because of their high nitrogen oxides and particulate emissions, this action, too, could further complicate automaker compliance with emissions standards.

Each of these problems/issues is discussed below in a way that highlights the potential opportunities and risks involved for both the auto industry and the federal government. Finally, the public policy questions that will have to be addressed in each of these situations in order to proactively manage such potentialities are set forth.

Use of Platinum-Group Metals

Based on the current state of the art in fuel management, the automotive industry is almost totally dependent on the utilization of PGMs as catalysts for emissions control. The platinum-group metals, or noble metals, have proved to be most advantageous catalytic agents for the oxidation and reduction of exhaust emissions because of their relatively low threshold activation temperature or light-off, fast warm-up, and ability to withstand thermal stresses. Though basic metals such as iron, nickel, vanadium, and titanium have been researched as potential catalytic substitutes they have not performed well in terms of activity, durability, and light-off temperature.

High-intensity ignition, better fuel evaporation methods, manifold preheat devices, modulated exhaust gas recirculation (EGR), and the catalytic converter are all employed in the new technology designed to improve fuel efficiency and minimize toxic substances in exhaust gas. However, the converter is the key element in pollution control to date, and without it fuel economy would flatten out at 14 miles per gallon. Since 1975 the oxidation converter, utilizing the catalysts platinum and palladium to convert hydrocarbons and carbon monoxide to carbon dioxide and water, has been standard on all cars. In 1981 nitrogen oxides will also have to be reduced (to 1.0 gram per mile), necessitating a reduction converter as well and the use of rhodium as a catalyst. A three-way catalytic converter will be used on all passenger cars (except diesel-, PROCO-, and CVCC-powered cars), requiring platinum and rhodium catalysts and an electronic-sensored fuel management system to achieve a stoichiometric air-fuel ratio.

However, before Detroit can supply all 1981 (and beyond) cars with the TWC, it must find a way to reduce the rhodium loading per TWC to within the mined ratio. Rhodium is a by-product of platinum mining and appears in a mined ratio of 18 to 19 parts platinum to 1 part rhodium, whereas the ratio of platinum to rhodium used in the TWC ranges from 7 to 1 to 12 to 1 (depending on the power train/TWC system being used). Needless to say, the auto industry is currently engaged in research in this area.

Converters can vary significantly in size (depending on vehicle size) and in structure (depending on manufacturer preference). General Motors uses a pelleted (PGM-coated) converter whereas Ford and Chrysler both use a monolithic honeycomb (dipped in PGM) version, each converter currently containing approximately 1 to 2 grams of precious metals. More than one converter can be used per car, often in tandem, with start-up, oxidation, and reduction converters expected to be common in a single vehicle after 1980. Use of PGM will increase through 1982-1983 with estimated loadings varying from a conservative 2.25 to 2.50 grams per car to double this figure, or 5 grams per car. Future cars will be smaller and lighter in weight, have smaller engine capacities, employ oxygen controls, and will eventually have improved engines and fuels which will virtually eliminate the need for catalytic converters (and will only require one small light-off oxidation catalyst).

Supply of Platinum-Group Metals

These metals come from several sources, as discussed below.

Domestic Resources. The United States is virtually dependent on imports for its PGM supply. Today it imports almost one-third of the world's total PGM production—33 percent from the Republic of South Africa; 29 percent from the Soviet Union; 23 percent from the United Kingdom, including Canada (essentially from South Africa); and 15 percent from other sources. It was estimated that in 1977 U.S. industries consumed (based on reported sales to industries) 1,650,000 troy ounces of PGMs (54 percent platinum, 40 percent palladium, 2 percent rhodium, and 4 percent other). With demand increasing at an annual rate of 5 percent, primarily because of increased demand by the auto industry as a result of emissions standards, further increases in the consumption of PGMs are expected through 1985. By that time, limited domestic resources may eventually be produced from the Stillwater Complex in Montana if environmental concerns can be resolved and if price economies warrant it. (Current estimates are that 100,000 troy ounces of platinum will be available at today's prices—$250 per ounce.)

It is interesting to note how PGM use has shifted. Prior to 1975 the U.S. chemical and electrical industries were the primary consumers of PGMs. With the installation of catalytic converters on U.S. passenger cars begun in that year, the automotive industry raced ahead of these industries in its demand for PGMs and by 1976 was purchasing 40 to 45 percent of all PGMs. In 1977 this increased to approximately 700,000 troy ounces—471,238 troy ounces of platinum and 192,000 troy ounces of palladium. Catalytic converters represent the largest single end use of PGM. The chemical and electrical industries are currently the next two largest U.S. consumers of PGMs—approximately 15 percent each.

Resources of the Republic of South Africa. This country produces approximately 61 percent of the world's supply of platinum (and has approximately 50 percent of total platinum resources). Palladium and rhodium are both by-products of platinum, but whereas palladium is present in the ore in a proportion of 2 parts platinum to 1 part palladium, rhodium, as noted earlier, is present in the proportion of 19 parts platinum to 1 part rhodium. This has major consequences for the auto industry and its ability to meet emissions standards after 1980, as will be discussed.

To keep the free market price of platinum in line with its expectations, South Africa cut back its production in late 1977, creating a price increase as well as a tight supply situation. Intermittent strikes in the country because of political/racial problems also created a tighter South African supply of platinum.

Resources of the Soviet Union. The Soviet Union produces approximately 31 percent of the world's platinum-group metals, most of it for export to Japan for the latter's jewelry industry (30 percent of world platinum consumption). However, in the Soviet Union platinum is present in ores in the approximate proportion of 2 parts palladium to 1 part platinum. The bulk of the country's PGM production is by-products of copper and nickel production and probably accounts for 40 percent of the world's resources. (The U.S.S.R. does not reveal such data.)

It appears that the Soviet Union ties its production and pricing of platinum to its grain crops—a good crop year means expensive platinum, a poor crop year means relatively cheap platinum. Historically, the Soviets have held back platinum sales in order to keep prices high and have increased sales when they need to buy grain with hard currency. (They are able to produce far more platinum than they need for their own industrial requirements.) Platinum exports from the Soviet Union have been down recently. This may be because the U.S.S.R. wants to create a price squeeze, or it may be because it is using platinum internally to manufacture Olympic coins.

Canadian Resources. These resources are directly tied to nickel and copper production since platinum is a by-product of these other metals. Because these metals' inventories have been substantially high recently, production has been down, thereby resulting in tighter platinum supplies. Canada produces about 10 percent of the world's supply of rhodium which appears in a ratio of approximately 7 to 1.

U.S. Stockpiles. Because the United States is so dependent on imports from South Africa and the Soviet Union, two areas where the political and economic ideologies often clash with those of the United States, and because the use of these metals is so vital to U.S. chemical production, petroleum refining, and medical industries, the U.S. General Services Administration (GSA) stockpiles platinum and palladium, but not rhodium, for strategic purposes. In 1977 its total inventory of platinum was 453,000 troy ounces, and the palladium inventory was 1,255,000 troy ounces. Goals for 1978 are to increase these to 1,314,000 troy ounces and 2,450,000 troy ounces, respectively.

The U.S. stockpile is sufficient for at least one year's consumption if that is limited to capital goods' strategic end uses (for example, in time of war, an embargo, prolonged strike, and so on). However, there is apparently also an additional three months' supply of platinum and a one year's supply of palladium which could be used for nonstrategic purposes, such as clean air. In addition, it is general knowledge that the private market (U.S. refiners, importers, dealers, and users such as the automotive industry) stockpiles at least twice as much as the U.S. government (although less than half of these stockpiles are actually reported), sufficient for one to two years of consumption.

According to 1978 Bureau of Mines data,[1] year-end refiner, importer, and dealer stocks have averaged over 1 million troy ounces for the last five years. Data reported by a precious-metals automotive industry expert indicate that the current (1975- through 1978-model years) average industry consumption level is approximately 370,000 troy ounces of PGM per model year. The Bureau of Mines reported automotive industry average PGM consumption during these same years as approximately 520,000 troy ounces. The difference of 150,000 troy ounces per year would indicate some stockpiling on the part of the auto industry. (The Bureau of Mines reported that PGM sales to the auto industry in 1977 were close to 480,000 troy ounces, reflecting an inventory drawdown on the stockpiles of 1975-1976. Moreover, the auto industry also reported private stockpiles of 1,012,812 troy ounces for 1977 to the Bureau of Mines.)

Therefore, general opinion seems to indicate that the United States possesses sufficient stocks of platinum and palladium to weather a short to medium interruption in supply (up to one year) without requiring substantial price increases. In addition, barring any major disruption of primary resources in the Republic of South Africa and/or the Soviet Union, world resources are apparently five to nine times the forecast demand for primary metals from 1977 to 2000.

Secondary Supply of PGM from Recycled Catalytic Converters. Another very important future source of PGM supply will be recycled converters. These should begin coming into scrapyards in 1981-1982 (approximately 5 percent of the cars reaching the yards will have had converters installed since 1975). Although it is somewhat questionable as to what percentage of PGM will be recoverable per vehicle, estimates range from 40 to 80 percent (based on the amount remaining in cars after 50,000-mile rugged durability tests). Precious-metals experts see no reason why 100 percent PGM will not actually be available for recycling in the future. They expect that 50 percent of cars first made with converters will be scrapped by 1985 and, therefore, that from 16 to 40 percent (maybe even 50 percent) PGM can be anticipated from recycled sources by 1985.

Other questions raised relative to PGM recycling include whether a system will be in place to handle the recycling of converters and whether the economics of that system will encourage scrapyard dealers to engage in this form of recycling. In answer to the first question, converter scrapping (and PGM recycling) will probably be centrally processed via existing networks which currently scrap radios, radiators, and so forth from passenger vehicles. As for the second question, because the process of collecting PGMs is not complicated (like collecting oil from oil changes) and could prove to be fairly remunerative, given the market price for precious metals as well as the automotive industry demand (a converter has a scrap value of approximately $12 based on current costs), not to mention the fact that the stainless-steel container holding the metals is probably as valuable to a scrap dealer as the PGM, the likelihood that scrapyard dealers would find this venture rather profitable runs high.

Risk Assessment of Impact of PGM Supply on the Automotive Industry

There are essentially two potential risks involved in terms of future PGM supply: the security of uninterrupted supplies from the Republic of South Africa and the Soviet Union at reasonable market prices and the availability of sufficient rhodium to comply with 1981 emissions standards.

Political instability and pressures on the United States to discontinue dealings with the Republic of South Africa have created some question as to the degree of certainty about future PGM supplies. According to metals industry experts as well as noted political strategists, a wholesale interruption of mine production and/or supply of metals from South Africa is not likely, except in the case of a large-scale war. What is more likely is that there will be minor interruptions in production caused by intermittent strikes. Pursuing the issue of the likelihood of political or racial upheaval, it is felt that South African guerilla forces are not yet sufficiently organized to use major aggression against their government, at least until the mid-1980s. Even then, rather than a major interruption in all mining production, the sabotage of individual mines appears more likely. Given fairly generous U.S. stocks, and the experts' "hiccup" theory that only minor, short-term interruptions are likely to occur relative to South Africa's PGM production and supply, it seems safe to assume that U.S. automakers will be able to obtain their PGM needs, at least through the 1980s.

The availability of sufficient rhodium to comply with 1981 U.S. passenger car standards, however, is dependent on the industry's ability to reduce rhodium loadings to within the mined ratio. If this is not done, the auto manufacturers may face a shortfall of rhodium because current supplies do not appear adequate for meeting future demand (1981). In addition, rhodium is only a by-product of platinum, South Africa's main market. Consequently, if the South Africans increase their rhodium production, they will also substantialy increase their platinum supply, thereby greatly depressing its market value and creating a surplus of other metal by-products as well (for example, palladium and iridium). For this reason South Africa is not likely to increase its platinum mining capacity to produce rhodium in the quantity needed by the U.S. auto industry—and rhodium prices will rise to a level that far exceeds economic practicability.

While the rhodium supply issue does seem to be critical, there is some feeling on the part of metals suppliers that because two and three catalytic converters will be used on all cars to improve fuel efficiency, the ratio of platinum to rhodium per vehicle will be in mined ratio. Moreover, GM and other technological experts have implied that great strides have been made in their research to reduce rhodium loadings, enhancing the likelihood of a breakthrough in this area, at least by 1981.

Emissions Control and the Diesel

In addition to the impact that an interruption in the supply of PGMs would have on the ability of the auto industry to meet future EPA standards, the risks involved in the diesel engine's ability to meet 1981 (and beyond) standards is also of great concern to the automakers.

The diesel engine is currently being tested as a possible danger to public health since diesel exhaust has been shown to contain thirty to ninety times more carbon particulates than gasoline-engine exhaust. Some scientists believe that these particulates can attach to the lung and may cause cancer. In addition, diesel manufacturers have not been able to control nitrogen oxides emissions below 1.5 grams per mile, thus adding the risk of diesel exhaust emissions. Still, the diesel engine does represent a proved technology that is more fuel-efficient than any other engine currently being produced. (General Motors' diesel engine has demonstrated a 30 percent improvement in fuel economy over comparably sized gasoline engines.)

Although the auto manufacturers can apply for a waiver on the 1981 nitrogen oxides standard for the diesel for four model years if no danger to public health is found, the diesel's future is highly uncertain at the moment. After the EPA announced the particulate standard in July 1978, California applied for and won approval of a lower nitrogen oxides exhaust (0.4 gram) by the 1982-model year, casting further doubt on the diesel and its availability to the auto industry for meeting corporate average fuel economy standards. To reduce particulates and nitrogen oxides emissions from the diesel exhaust will require complete redesign of the engine's combustion chamber, a process that may take too long for the industry to accomplish in order to meet regulatory emissions and fuel economy standards in 1981 and beyond.

Public Policy Options

The issues discussed relative to the risks involved with PGM supply and the diesel-powered engine cry out for some rationality and cooperation between the auto industry and the regulators, and specifically for federal policy guidelines concerning these matters. Barring alternative technological breakthroughs by 1981, some options that should be considered are:

Accepting the shortcomings of higher levels of emissions or fuel economy until technology is able to relieve such problems as rhodium loading and diesel-engine nitrogen oxides emissions

Changing the U.S. emissions measurement system so that it is more like Japan's

Promoting federal funding of automaker research into alternative technologies to create a "strategic technology reserve"

Establishing compensatory tax treatment, at either the manufacturer or consumer level, to offset any higher costs of alternative technologies

Launching a major federal rhodium stockpiling program at public expense

Permitting some specific mix of gasoline and diesel engines in each manufacturer's output, thereby creating a fleet average emissions standard

The shortcomings of these options can obviously be overcome through some relaxation in federal standards, by giving additional responsibility to the consumer for subsidizing clean air, and through more collaboration between regulators and the auto industry to develop economical and practicable solutions to the problems involved.

American Motors Corporation

As with safety, AMC does very little basic research in the area of emissions control and, as a matter of practical policy, does not engage in any independent research but works together with a few carburetor and electronics suppliers, focusing efforts on improving engine carburetion and applying electronics technology to engine developments.

The core of the engine line for AMC's passenger cars in the 1980s will be a newly developed 2.5-liter four-cylinder engine developed and supplied by Pontiac. Consequently, for most of its emissions technology AMC will again be dependent on GM.

At present AMC is not undertaking research of any importance relative to diesel engines and dieselization. Diesels could become important to AMC, especially for improving the fuel economy of its nonpassenger vehicles. However, considering the uncertain outcome of regulations on nitrogen oxides emissions, AMC has opted to depend on the diesel research done by other manufacturers. If regulations permit the use of diesel engines, AMC could procure these from GM or possibly from Renault.

American Motors Corporation uses catalytic converters to improve the emissions of its engines and plans to use a three-way catalyst to meet future emissions standards. Consequently, an interruption in the supply of platinum and rhodium would immediately affect its ability to comply with the federal standards. Nevertheless, AMC's concerns do not center as much on the availability of these metals as on their price. A likely scenario is that a brief interruption in the supply of noble metals would be followed by a drastically changed pricing situation. A long-term suspension of the supply of the noble metals seems unlikely, however, since this would not be in the interest of the principal suppliers.

American Motors Corporation feels that some sort of federal stockpiling program would help to bridge a brief interruption in supply, but in the case of a longer interruption or a dramatic increase in price, this kind of government assistance could not remedy the situation. A particularly frightening scenario for AMC is one where it would be forced to fully absorb a price increase. In all AMC's market segments it looks to GM as its price leader. Of course, GM, having far greater capability to absorb cost increases, might choose to do so rather than passing them on to the consumer.

In summary, if the price of noble metals were to increase drastically, some sort of tradeoff between emissions and fuel economy standards would have to be made in order to avoid a further deterioration of the competitive situation in the auto industry.

Chrysler Corporation

Chrysler was a late convert to the catalytic converter because of its doubts about the effectiveness of the concept. Its concerns centered on the reliability of catalytic converters and their excessive heat buildup which could represent potential fire hazards. Instead, Chrysler opted to "clean up" the engine from within through the use of electronic technology. In 1975 the company introduced an electronic lean-burn system that electronically controls the air-fuel ratio. By 1977, however, this system alone was not sufficient to meet stricter fuel emissions standards, and Chrysler started to equip its cars with catalytic converters as well. Meanwhile, GM and Ford had already introduced the oxidation converter in their cars, and Chrysler's initial fears had turned out to be unfounded. To meet future emissions standards, Chrysler is expected to use an improved version of its electronic fuel control system in combination with a three-way catalytic converter.

The uncertainty surrounding federal standards on nitrogen oxides and particulates emissions has kept Chrysler from investing heavily in diesel research. The feeling is that in this uncertain situation only GM may be able to achieve enough volume of diesel engines to recoup its investment and attain a profit before new standards effectively rule out the use of diesels. However, if Chrysler were to introduce a diesel engine, it would probably have to absorb a loss in the event that the regulations change. Nevertheless, Chrysler's engineers keep up with any progress in diesel technology so that, if the uncertainty is removed, the company will have the expertise to dieselize one of its current engines.

Because Chrysler uses catalytic converters to reduce exhaust pollution, its continuing compliance with emissions standards will depend on the availability of the platinum-group metals used as catalysts. If for some reason platinum metals were not available, Chrysler would have to either break the law or stop production. However, to the extent that all manufacturers would be equally affected by an interruption in the platinum supply or a sudden and sharp increase in the price of PGMs, Chrysler does not see this as a strategic issue. (Within the company only those issues that affect Chrysler's relative competitive position are viewed as strategic issues.) Moreover, because the cost of noble metals used in the converter is still only a fraction of the total cost of the converter system, a price increase in these metals would not have a noticeable impact on Chrysler's profit margins.

If the supply of platinum-group metals were to be interrupted for a prolonged period, Chrysler feels that this would create a situation where the federal government would have to take steps to ensure that the industry is able to continue to operate.

Ford Motor Company

Although the potential risks discussed earlier apply to Ford as well as to the other automakers, in general PGM supply does not really seem to be a critical issue for the company. The reasons for this are as follows.

1. Ford has entered into relatively stable long-term contracts with Rustenberg Mines for its PGM supply. In addition, because Ford supplies only its own vehicles (GM also supplies AMC) and produces 40 percent fewer vehicles than GM, its total supply needs are probably half those of GM. Therefore, even if any South African turmoil were to cause a short- to medium-term supply interruption, Ford would not be likely to experience a critical PGM shortfall.

2. Ford is relatively optimistic that a PGM alternative—a basic metal catalyst—will become available by 1985. While PGM supply may not be a real problem, Ford (and the other automakers) is actively pursuing alternatives to PGMs for cost-cutting purposes.

3. Along with other package efficiencies, Ford has the potential advantage in the PROCO engine which, when available, will require only an oxidation converter and not a three-way catalytic device.

Ford was not in a particularly viable financial position in 1974-1975 to invest in the diesel engine (as GM was able to do). In addition, it was already committed to heavy investment in the PROCO engine development. Now, when its financial position has become brighter, questions relating to the diesel's ability to pass particulate and stringent nitrogen oxides emissions standards, its relatively poor performance characteristics (relative to the traditional gasoline Otto cycle), and its potential for greater manufacturer product-liability exposure (because of carcinogens) have dampened Ford's interest in aggressively investing in diesel development. However, Ford does have an ongoing diesel research program, and if future emissions standards permit diesel use, Ford is sure to go ahead with diesel production. Its engine R&D data clearly indicate the advantages (and probable necessity) of using the diesel to gain the last 2 to 3 miles per gallon for meeting the 1985 (27.5 miles per gallon) standards and may figure importantly in dealing with any more stringent post-1985 standards.

General Motors Corporation

General Motors is concerned about apparent PGM supply shortages and primarily about what appears to be an insufficient supply of rhodium to meet 1981 passenger car nitrogen oxides emissions standards of 1.0 gram per mile. Recently GM's supplier told the company that it can only expect to receive 25,000 ounces of rhodium annually, which is approximately one-quarter of GM's projected need in 1981, assuming that the three-way converter currently being developed is successful.

Assuming that GM begins to stockpile rhodium now at the rate of 25,000 ounces per year, its reserve in 1981 (when the 1.0 gram standard for nitrogen oxides takes effect) would be 75,000 ounces—not enough to meet one full year's need. At 0.016 ounce of rhodium per converter and a volume of, say, 6 million U.S. passenger vehicles, GM would need approximately 96,000 ounces in 1981 alone and a similar amount in 1982, but would have only 100,000 ounces available in 1981 and 25,000 ounces in 1982. However, in the course of our conversations GM has said that the company is not seriously concerned with rhodium supply up to 1982. Presumably, the required annual purchases noted could be provided from company stockpiles. General Motors feels that the supply situation will become more difficult after 1982.

General Motors has two major concerns with regard to the nitrogen oxides emissions standard, namely:

1. Every vehicle GM currently produces with a catalytic converter is tied to a single source, and that source is in a militarily and politically vulnerable part of the world (South Africa).
2. General Motors' currently guaranteed supply of rhodium is not nearly sufficient to meet its volume needs, given known emissions control technology.

As a matter of public policy GM has taken the position vis-à-vis future emissions standards that the federal nitrogen oxides standard should not be as stringent as the California standard (that is, that the government should adopt a two-car standard, one for California and one for the rest of the country, of not less than 1.5 grams per mile) and that the EPA should restudy the issue of PGM supply before establishing 1981 industry emissions standards.

With regard to the question of diesels, GM has repeatedly stated that technically it cannot meet a national nitrogen oxides emissions standard of 1.0 gram per mile, much less the 0.4 gram per mile standard in California. Because the company has projected as much as a 25 percent share of the market for the fuel-saving diesels by 1985, and plans to produce them in a V-8 configuration (to replace existing V-8 gasoline engines) as well as in at least one smaller configuration, it would prefer to see the government give an exception to diesels on nitrogen oxides emissions as well as particulates—at least until a new technology that will meet government regulations for gasoline engines is visible.

Toyota Motor Company

To meet Japan's 1978 emissions standards, Toyota has adopted the use of (1) three-way catalysts for cars with engine sizes of 2,000 cubic centimeters or larger; (2) a combination of a lean air-fuel mixture combustion system and an oxidation catalyst for cars with engine sizes between 1,500 and 1,800 cubic centimeters; and (3) an oxidation catalyst for 1,300-cubic centimeters cars.

Given a scenario where platinum supplies are unavailable, Toyota's prognosis is as follows:

1. It would probably not be able to use catalytic converters. Thus, controlled combustion would be the only alternative.

2. The effectiveness of controlled combustion technologies would depend on vehicle weight.

3. Because controlled combustion does not allow an optimally efficient air-fuel ratio, fuel efficiency would suffer considerably, making compliance with fuel economy standards difficult. The larger the car, the more difficulties created by a lean-burn engine.

4. Controlled combustion may not allow all the emissions requirements to be met.

5. Consequently, the government would have to make tradeoff decisions between fuel economy and emissions control. Toyota believes that in such an instance fuel economy should be emphasized since energy is the bigger of the two problems.

As for diesel cars, Toyota's commitment to date has been relatively minor so that the question of potentially tighter emissions controls on diesel cars is not a serious concern. Since 1977 Toyota has been marketing a diesel version of the Crown with a 2.2-liter four-cylinder engine. The 2.2-liter engine is the smallest diesel engine that Toyota has. It was developed as an all-purpose engine and can be mounted on small trucks. Despite the high initial cost of diesel cars, the fuel economy they offer and the Japanese government's policy of keeping diesel fuel inexpensive could stimulate sales of diesel cars in the Japanese domestic market.

Whether the diesel Crown and its relatively large engine/car size—two attributes that are more suited to the taxi market—would appeal to the average private car buyer is yet to be seen. Depending on the market results, Toyota may expand its commitment to diesel cars and, consequently, is viewing Volkswagen's 1,600-cubic-centimeter diesel Rabbit with considerable interest. However, the Japanese government has implied that if Toyota should develop and market a large number of small diesel cars suited for the mass private ownership market, it would be compelled to apply to those cars the same emissions standards already applied to gasoline passengar cars. Moreover, it is assumed that if Toyota markets such a car, the rest of the industry will follow suit, thereby resulting in a large diesel car population on the Japanese roads and the certain application of stringent standards.

Current diesel technology cannot meet any emissions control regulations that are more severe than 1.0 gram per mile of nitrogen oxides. It is therefore up to the governments of Japan and, particularly, the United States to choose the appropriate role and objective for the diesel car to meet—fuel economy or emissions control. Particulates are another major unresolved issue. Toyota is currently taking a wait-and-see approach to determine whether the U.S. consumer will take to diesel cars by choosing fuel efficiency and accepting the accompanying odor and vibrations. To the extent that General Motors will depend on diesel cars (up to 25 percent) to meet the 1985 U.S. fuel economy fleet average requirement, this appears to Toyota to be as key a question as that of future emissions control standards.

At this point Toyota has no plans to introduce its diesel cars into the U.S. market, although this policy may change in the future.

Nissan Motor Company

Japan's emissions control standards have increasingly become more stringent. To meet the 1975 standards, Nissan concluded that the catalytic system would be the most advantageous overall solution to its varied engine sizes after evaluating the control capabilities, fuel efficiency, and driveability effects of the system. The application thus consisted of a combination of (1) improvements in the existing reciprocating engine to add a lean-burn characteristic so as to achieve both fuel efficiency and reductions of burden on the catalytic converter; (2) exhaust gas recirculation (EGR) to reduce nitrogen oxides emissions; and (3) the use of an oxidation catalyst to reduce hydrocarbons and carbon monoxide, plus secondary air infusion for promoting oxidation by the catalyst.

In meeting the 1976 standards, Nissan's approach to further reduce nitrogen oxides emissions involved increasing the EGR ratio by adding a mechanism to control EGR in relation to the engine's particular driving state. Subsequently, to clear the 1978 standards, Nissan adopted a combination of (1) the three-way catalyst; (2) a fast-burn engine system (NAPS-Z) plus EGR for the control of nitrogen oxides; and (3) an improved oxidation catalyst. An oxygen sensor mechanism was also used in the three-way catalyst system. Essentially, the three-way catalyst is applied to Nissan's larger-sized models, the NAPS-Z to the medium-range models (for example, the Bluebird and the Skyline), and the improved oxidation catalyst to the smallest models that generally have engines smaller than 1,500 cubic centimeters. Nissan's R&D expenditures during FY 1977 totaled approximately $250 million, a large portion of which was used to meet the emissions control standards.

When the nitrogen oxides emissions standard of 1.0 gram per mile goes into effect in the United States, Nissan will essentially rely on the three-way catalyst with an electronic control mechanism on the engine and the fast-burn engine system (or NAPS-Z) in order to secure fuel efficiency. The fast-burn engine system is designed to operate around the stoichiometric air-fuel ratio to achieve fuel efficiency and driveability, and simultaneously large EGR to suppress the generation of nitrogen oxides. In order to counteract the tendency for unstable combustion resulting from large EGR, a fast-burn process is promoted by using two spark plugs.

The scenario of a possible cutoff in platinum supplies has been incorporated into Nissan's R&D programs. In this case fuel efficiency would drastically suffer, and the fleet average mileage figure could never approach anything like 27.5 miles per gallon. The drop in efficiency could be as much as 20 to 30 percent. For Nissan the probable alternative to a platinum catalyst would be a thermal reactor. The very core of technical thinking at Nissan, however, seems to revolve around the view that—whether the platinum-based catalyst or the thermal reactor—these approaches involve creating a burning process outside the engine, and therefore that it would be far more sensible to look for solutions where all the burning is done within the engine.

Nissan has the longest history of all the Japanese automakers in marketing diesel passenger cars, even though the scale of its involvement has been limited. The company began such a program in the mid-1960s largely for export purposes. (Note that Japan's taxi market has been dominated by gasoline-engined vehicles converted to burn liquefied petroleum gas.) The initial shipments of Nissan diesel cars with 2-liter engines were all destined for Hong Kong's taxi market; export shipments to Scandinavia followed. Only afterward did some domestic sales start, but still only two taxi companies had bought diesel cars.

After the energy crisis, interest in diesel passenger cars began to increase in Japan, and the general public started to take note of their advantages. Most buyers of diesel cars are people who drive long distances and farmers who are accustomed to buying inexpensive diesel fuel to run their farm equipment. Thus, the acceptance of diesel cars first began in the northern island of Hokkaido where a comparatively large land area for the size of the population created both conditions—long travel distances and large farms.

The popularity of diesel cars is currently spreading to the rest of the country since one attraction of diesel cars is the fact that for the same amount it takes to purchase and operate a gasoline-engined car, a larger, diesel-engined car can be bought. Although the initial purchase price of a diesel car is higher, its lower maintenance costs and fuel costs even out, to make the total cost about equal to that of owning a smaller gasoline car. Diesel cars tend to be large in the spectrum of various cars produced in Japan. Nissan's earlier diesel cars featured a 2.0-liter engine, which has been recently supplemented by a 2.2-liter engine.

Nissan recognizes the attributes of Volkswagen's 1,600-cubic-centimeter diesel Rabbit in terms of improved performance and comfort features, and the fact that VW has managed to lower the price by producing diesel engines which share parts and the production process used in its gasoline engine production. Nissan is particularly intrigued by the fact that this development occurred in Germany where the price of diesel fuel is not any cheaper than that of gasoline.

Nissan recognizes the inherent significance of the diesel's potential in Japan, even more than in the United States, since Japan's energy problems are by far more serious. The use of diesel engines has steadily expanded over the years in the truck sector, and the same could happen in the passenger car sector. Before this can happen, however, some noise and vibration problems must be solved. With the increased R&D efforts expected to take place at Nissan, good results are likely to be obtained that could make Nissan's (and other Japanese) diesel cars even more comfortable than the Mercedes-Benz. One major concern in this regard, however, is future developments in diesel-related emissions control regulations. If the number of diesel cars does proliferate, the Japanese government may change its current practice of classifying diesel cars with trucks and apply standards that are closer or equal to passenger car emissions control standards. Today's diesel is not capable of meeting the kind of nitrogen oxides standards (0.4 gram per mile) that passenger cars must meet in Japan.

To date, Nissan's commitment to diesel passenger cars has been limited, and the market response, although increasing, is difficult to assess. However, the company is assuming a flexible posture as it continues to weigh the inherently large potential that diesel technology could have as well as the possibility of stricter emissions control standards.

Honda Motor Company

Honda's efforts to achieve its fuel efficiency objectives will be complicated if the United States eventually applies a nitrogen oxides standard of 0.4 gram per mile, even though such a standard went into effect in Japan during 1978. Honda's concern stems from the fact that the difference in the test modes used in the two countries will make meeting the U.S. comparable numerical standard more difficult.

Honda's CVCC engine is functioning well. In principle, the CVCC engine could be applied to larger engines beyond those the company now produces—with considerable certainty up to 2.8-liter engines. In fact, Honda has converted a number of V-8 engines, displacing more than 300 cubic inches, thus demonstrating the applicability of the CVCC system to larger engines. In order to clear Japan's 1978 emissions control standards and to simultaneously achieve a favorable fuel economy level and driveability characteristics, Honda's CVCC engine has been coupled with a thermal reactor. Catalysts, however, are not used.

Honda's initial hesitancy in using catalytic converters has proved to be unwarranted. Thus far the company has pursued alternatives to the catalytic converter because little has been known about the potential problems related to the device. These potential problems include possible new difficulties that the by-products of the chemical process might generate (for example, sulfur dioxide, polynuclear aromatic, and so on); the reliability of the continued effectiveness of the catalytic converter through the life of a car; and uncertainty about the method of reclaiming platinum and the future availability of this metal. These concerns are turning out to be much less serious than originally thought. Therefore, there is a possibility that Honda may utilize an oxidation catalyst in addition to the CVCC. In meeting stricter emissions control standards in the United States, Honda may find such an approach more conducive in terms of fuel efficiency objectives. At any rate, inclusion of an oxidation catalyst among the acceptable alternatives wil allow Honda greater flexibility in seeking a combined solution to emissions control, fuel efficiency, and driveability and comfort objectives. The company, however, has not relaxed its caution in regard to the three-way catalyst because it believes that so far nothing has been proved about such potential problems as the generation of ammonia and cyanide as well as the lasting reliability of the device.

The hypothetical situation of a cutoff in platinum supplies would require Honda to make a tradeoff between emissions control and fuel efficiency. To the extent that the company plans to use oxidation catalysts to obtain both high emissions control capabilities and good fuel efficiency, it would also face this tradeoff dilemma. Moreover, its current search for alternative methods that includes a scenario where platinum is not available to deal with these two dual objectives plus the driveability objective would be made meaningless if the United States eventually chose to apply a higher emissions control standard for nitrogen oxides of 0.4 gram per mile.

Honda is very interested in using the diesel engine in passenger cars, but current uncertainties preclude it from commercializing at this point. The uncertainties essentially consist of the following. First, if more stringent emissions control requirements are imposed on the diesel passenger car, the diesel will lose its inherent advantage. The existing technology enables control of nitrogen oxides at 1.0 to 1.5 grams per mile at the maximum.

Second, a great deal more needs to be known about how to deal with the problems of particulates emissions, smoke, odor, sulfur oxides, noise, and vibrations.

Third, major advancements being made in the fuel efficiency of the gasoline engine are eating into the advantages of the diesel engine. In addition, the production of diesel cars would require major retooling expenses, and the diesel car itself would be heavier than a gasoline car. Therefore, Honda is not currently convinced that the money and time required to refine diesel technology might not be better spent on the gasoline-engine option.

Volkswagen AG

In a scenario where the availability of platinum and rhodium is limited, VW's ability to meet emissions control standards would depend primarily on the length of the shortage as well as the success of its own efforts to develop and test technical alternatives to the current catalyst systems that rely on noble metals. In contrast to some U.S. automakers, VW has no precious-metals trading activity of its own. Instead, it appears to have special long-term contracts with leading international metal traders who stock metals for the company and apparently guarantee delivery. These suppliers are Degussa AG[2] (Frankfurt), Johnson & Mathey (London), and Engelhardt Industries (United States). The supply pipeline from South Africa to VW (via these metal traders) apparently has sufficient inventory that VW regards short-term and even medium-term supply bottlenecks as unlikely.

Volkswagen's forecast of 25 percent diesel-engined cars in its U.S. sales mix will significantly increase its emissions control problems. The company maintains that a target of 2.0 grams per mile for nitrogen oxides is easily attainable and that it can also match the 1.5-gram target with its current technology, but that it cannot match the 1.0-gram target set for 1981 and beyond. As for the 0.4 gram per mile nitrogen oxides "research goal," VW regards this as unattainable for diesel engines. The company's future emphasis on turbocharged diesels to attain performance improvements will further increase the nitrogen oxides emissions problem.

Although all large chemicals companies are working on new converter technologies (in Germany these include Degussa, Hoechst, BASF, and Bayer), VW does not expect a breakthrough in the foreseeable future, and probably not before 1983 or 1985. The most promising alternative development to date appears to be the Bosch system that uses an exhaust sensor device and a closed-loop technology based on a complex electronic control system. This development, however, is still far from attaining the 1981 and later emissions standards.

Volkswagen's technical staff is fully absorbed in its efforts to meet the 1981 and later emissions standards by refining current three-way catalytic converter technologies. As already noted, the company views the probability of shortages in the supply of noble metals as small. If a short-term supply bottleneck should occur, VW would expect significant price increases of $20 to $30. However, in view of the small amount of noble metals used to produce a single converter, this price increase is not expected to influence the overall price of a car significantly. Similarly, VW does not expect the administration to grant a significant waiver of emissions control standards in the event of such a shortage.

It is important to note that the vast majority of VW's total production sold outside the United States (approximately 85 percent) is not equipped with catalytic converters. Because there is no indication that converters will become mandatory in major European markets within the foreseeable future, VW's probable response to more stringent U.S. emissions standards (nitrogen oxides of 1.0 and 0.4 gram) will probably be an involuntary deemphasis in U.S. market sales because any vehicles not in compliance with U.S. regulations would not be permitted into the country.

In summary, then, a shortage of noble metals would not be expected to influence VW's ability to respond to existing emissions standards. In the unlikely event that such a shortage were long term (more than one year) or that more stringent standards are issued which cannot be met with the available technology, VW would probably shift its emphasis away from the United States. It does not expect new technologies that are needed to substitute (partly) for the noble metals and/or meet increased standards to be available within the next few years.

Notes

1. *Mineral Commodity Summaries*, 1978, U.S. Department of the Interior, Bureau of Mines.

2. Degussa is considered to be a European leader in the development of catalytic converters, having started its research work in 1961.

Part II
Pricing Policy

Pricing Policy as a Factor in
Regulatory Decision Making

Automotive regulatory requirements have costs attached to them. Determining the magnitude of these costs is a task of considerable complexity, and one that has already generated debate and controversy.[1] It is not within the scope of this book to arrive at a definitive dollar amount attributable to government regulation or to argue the perceived or social value of safety or emissions standards. Rather, it is our intent to assess the impact of regulatory content on the pricing policy of the automakers. This regulatory content cost has a twofold significance.

1. *It is, in itself, a relatively large amount.* Assuming no offsetting *economies* in cost generated by federal requirements, no less than 8 percent of the price of a $5,000 automobile is attributable to regulatory content.

2. *It has the potential of distorting relative pricing patterns.* The unit costs associated with most U.S. government regulatory requirements implemented through the 1978-model year appear to be fairly similar, whether the vehicles involved are large and luxurious or small and spartan. If the automakers were to pass such costs through uniformly in their pricing, this would tend to make small, spartan cars progressively more costly in relationship to large, luxurious ones.

Clearly, regulatory policymakers, if they are to pursue their legislated missions responsibly, must understand the pricing philosophies and policies of the automakers as best they can, regardless of whether they sympathize with them.

Of particular importance in regulatory policy is the issue of economic practicability. The Energy Policy and Conservation Act of 1975 explicitly stipulates that economic practicability be employed as a rule-making criterion. Incremental costs surely impact manufacturer pricing decisions, although not necessarily immediately and directly on actual car prices. Nonetheless, to the degree that incremental costs flowing from regulatory requirements are passed through to consumers in pricing, there is a wide spectrum of possible economic impact. The extremes of that spectrum might be characterized as follows:

Consumers could perceive the benefits associated with new regulatory requirements to be much greater to them than the associated cost increment, both in immediate terms and over the total ownership period of their automobiles. This sense of higher value could conceivably enhance sales volumes and, in turn, benefit the entire economy.

Consumers could perceive virtually no benefit to them of regulatory requirements. Consequently, any large price increases they might confront (arising from the combination of regulation and inflation) could lead them to either postpone purchasing decisions or change historic buying patterns. In other words, demand may prove price to be significantly elastic.

Regulatory decisions, alone, will shape neither consumer behavior nor the financial future of the automakers and their circles of economic impact. As the magnitude of these decisions grows, however, they are becoming progressively more influential, and most probably will be the leading factors impacting both of these elements during the next five years.

The Sensitivity of Pricing Policy

Pricing is one of the most privileged forms of managerial decision making in any company. The criteria that go into pricing determinations, the process by which pricing decisions are made, and the human dynamics applied to that process are all matters of extreme privacy. In a complex, broadly influential industry with a sizable number of different and large product/market segments, as the auto-motive industry, the confidentiality of the pricing process is a particularly sensitive issue.

This concern must surely be heightened by the implications of the current action being taken by the FTC against four large cereal manufacturers. If this action is decided in favor of the FTC, it would mean that any highly concentrated industry could be exposed to antitrust charges based primarily on degree of concentration.

Finally, automotive pricing policy is an area where virtually all generalizations are subject to exception. This, in itself, leads to the conclusion—and, we believe, an appropriate one—that pricing has a substantial judgmental quality which is probably much greater than people outside the industry realize.

A further complication in commenting on pricing policy in the automotive industry is due to the fact that it is an area replete with disagreement. This disagreement takes many forms:

Intramural disagreement. Different functions within the same company, most notably sales and finance, may display considerably diverging philosophies on what shape a pricing policy should take.

Intermural disagreement. One company's perception of the pricing policy of a competitor may not match that competitor's view of his own actions.

Observer disagreement. Complete outsiders (including government policy-makers) appear to view pricing policy in ways that diverge strongly from how the automakers perceive the practical realities.

Intent of This Document

No truly comprehensive and authoritative commentary could conceivably be developed on the subject of pricing policy in the U.S. automotive industry by an outsider. Moreover, it is quite likely that no such commentary could be developed even by an industry insider. Part of this difficulty stems from the previously mentioned judgmental quality of many pricing decisions; another part stems from the incompleteness, even in companies as vast as the leading automakers, of data on which pricing decisions are based.

With this in mind, our goal here is to portray as best we can many of the major influences on automotive pricing; the ways in which these influences seem to have been integrated into pricing decisions; and the likely path that pricing philosophy may follow in the future, given the most visible, predictable new forces with which the automakers must contend.

Note

1. The 1978 *Automotive News Annual* reports that the retail price of an average 1978-model passenger car has been impacted $666 by federal requirements instituted since 1968. Of this amount, $430 is attributed to safety regulations; the remaining $236 is accounted for primarily by emissions control equipment. The National Highway Traffic Safety Administration takes strong exception to the $430 figure, asserting that the cost of safety and damageability standards over this period has been $250 per car, or 42 percent lower than the figure reported in *Automotive News.* If one accepts the NHTSA figure and adds it to the $236 for nonsafety regulations, the total cost per car of government regulations can be estimated at $486, or nearly 10 percent of the price of a $5,000 automobile. If one accepts the NHTSA figure and reduces the nonsafety amount by a comparable 42 percent, the total cost per car of government regulations is $387, or nearly 8 percent of the price of a $5,000 automobile.

4 Aggregate Demand

Demand Correlations

Over much of the past three decades there has been a fairly consistent secular correlation between dollars spent on new cars and personal consumption expenditures. Typically, new-car purchases have accounted for approximately 4.5 percent of the personal consumption index (PCI). (In recent years it would appear that this has been declining toward approximately 4.2 percent. However, we believe that if the recent surge in purchases of light commercial vehicles for noncommercial uses were to be factored in—essentially generating the sale of approximately 1.5 million additional "pseudo cars" in 1977—the 4.5 percent figure would be reestablished.)

In a broad sense, 4.5 percent of PCI represents roughly, in retail revenue terms, the potential market available to the automakers. Lately, the downward sensitivity from this guideline figure has been very great. For example, in 1970, with the long strike at General Motors, and in 1974-1975, with the backwash of the Arab oil embargo, new-car purchases dropped to only about 3.0 percent of PCI.

Achieving this market potential is a critical managerial goal for the auto industry because it is so highly labor-intensive. At General Motors, for example, employee compensation accounts for 35 cents of each dollar of cost and is surpassed in dollar value only by purchases from vendors. Under the collective bargaining agreements that exist between the United Automobile Workers and the automakers, labor must be considered at least a semifixed expense. When viewed together with other fixed and semifixed expenses, this creates a set of financial dynamics in which company efforts to sustain high sales volume levels and to capture 4.5 percent of PCI become vital.

The natural interest of the auto companies in realizing full market potential coincides with the interests of other influential institutions. With two-thirds of all new passenger cars being purchased on credit terms, automobile credit remains the largest single component of overall consumer credit—27 percent during the 1970s. As sales weakened in 1974, the financial institutions themselves acted to buoy their own business (and, in turn, that of the automakers) by offering for the first time credit terms of up to forty-eight months on a widespread, widely advertised basis. According to the Federal Reserve Bulletin, by 1976 more than one-third of all automotive installment paper was for terms of more than thirty-six months. Interestingly, the fact that approximately one out of every four new-car buyers is paying for that car over a four-year period has not disturbed long-term ownership practices. The average first-owner period of ownership remains at the same three-year level that has prevailed throughout most of the postwar period.

Elasticity

In Robert F. Lanzillotti's article "The Automotive Industry," published in *The Structure of American Industry*, six estimates of elasticity of new-car purchases with respect to price and income are discussed. Two of these were developed prior to World War II and the remaining four in 1957-1958. All conclude that there is a considerably higher responsiveness of demand to changes in individual income than to changes in price. Using one of the middle-range sets of elasticity estimates, that produced by Gregory C. Chow, Lanzillotti projects, for example, that the downward influence on unit sales of a 5 percent increase in price would be wholly offset by a 2 percent increase in personal income. Similarly, a 5 percent increase in price coinciding with a 4 percent increase in income would generate a 6 percent growth in demand.

These analyses suggest that in a period of inflation, such as the past decade, if disposable personal income were to rise at a faster rate than new-car prices, continued growth in demand would probably be supported. In fact, during the past decade per capita disposable personal income did increase at an average rate slightly higher than 8.0 percent. The Department of Labor's price index for new cars (which is adjusted to compensate for improvements in value) reflected an average annual increase for the same period of 3.5 percent. Without any adjustment it would appear that new-car prices in the United States increased at an average rate of around 6.0 percent.

Therefore, the pricing behavior of the automakers seems to be equally consistent with their own interests in attempting to ensure high volume levels as well as with the conclusions drawn by the economists whose works are cited by Lanzillotti.

5 Factors in Pricing Policy

Volume Orientation

The primacy of volume orientation in the U.S. automotive industry is an early thread in its history. United States automakers concede that they were good designers, manufacturers, and salespeople well before they became equally skilled financial managers. This volume-oriented tradition and the use of aggressive pricing as a means of achieving it were cited prominently in a 1939 Federal Trade Commission investigation of the industry.

Although theoretical studies of elasticity indicate that automotive demand is not extremely sensitive to price increases, the penalties of being wrong in this regard (that is, of overpricing and seeing this demand seriously cut) are extremely high. According to the estimates of industry analyst Arvid Jouppi, General Motors' profit declines two-and-one-half times as fast as any decline in unit volume. Jouppi's estimate for Ford is even higher, three times, and for Chrysler he estimates it to be four times. Consequently, there are probably stronger tendencies to underprice than overprice.

An additional force which moves the U.S. automakers toward a high-volume orientation is the Japanese auto companies. Japanese enterprises are growth-fixated to an even greater extent than U.S. companies. In pursuit of the most rapid growth possible, they have shown a great willingness to invest large sums to build up a strong position in a major market such as the United States.

The Product Planning Process

Pricing goals are determined early in the process by which new products are developed in the automobile manufacturing companies. These price targets are established largely on the basis of past experience and expectations of future buyer behavior. Although a considerable amount of data is fed into the planning judgments on price, final decisions appear to be wholly judgmental.

As the product planning process begins, efforts are made to characterize proposed new products and, based on market research and expected trends in consumer behavior, to estimate sales levels at different possible prices. These, combined with estimates of unit cost at different sales levels, provide a view of potential profitability in terms of both return on sales (ROS) and return on investment (ROI). A favorable product profit perspective, particularly one that extends over a wide range of variables, would naturally encourage corporate decisionmakers. However, once a product concept is approved and begins moving toward realization, the original financial planning assumptions—its financial frame of reference—may change. Newer market research and newly forming trends in consumer behavior may influence sales forecasts upward or downward; new cost experience may shift cost estimates in either direction. At different stages in the product development cycle, different options are open to the automakers for responding to new data—especially unfavorable data—ranging from substantial and organic changes early in the development cycle to relatively cosmetic changes late in the cycle. Product developers strive to take actions that will maintain or improve the "financials" which led them to make the "go" decision in the first place. The financial criteria employed in these continual reevaluations are quite formal. The data applied to them are a mix of current data and managerial judgments of how the future will affect those data.

The current cycle of product planning stretches over more than five years and involves a continuous iteration which forces original pricing decisions through a long series of intrafunctional debates. Throughout the process the automakers constantly address a central judgmental issue: How much will the public pay for a vehicle of the character being developed?

The product planning process, as carried out at Ford Motor Company, is typical enough in its flow to illustrate the process followed by U.S. automakers generally. At Ford, three groups are involved.

1. *Corporate Strategy and Alternatives Group.* This centralized staff function is charged with defining new product line needs and broadly characterizing each proposed new product line in terms of characteristics and market. The latter task includes estimating the pricing levels required to meet market objectives for the proposed new product. Typically, the group prepares alternative strategies for any intended new product program (as many as four, and each with a number of variations) for review by the Office of the Chief Executive.

2. *North American Automotive Operations (NAAO).* This line organization reviews the product program alternative chosen by the Office of the Chief Executive from those submitted by the Corporate Strategy and Alternatives Group and subjects it to intensive analysis for feasibility and appropriateness. Pricing assumptions are an important element of this analysis. The NAAO endeavors to determine which alternative strategy seems most desirable. It then makes any modifications in the product concept it deems necessary and approves the concept for further development efforts.

3. *Advanced Vehicle Development Group.* This centralized staff activity is hardware- rather than concept-oriented. It takes the product concept and converts it to a set of detailed performance specifications—dimensions, weight requirements, styling renderings, component analyses (especially to determine which major components will have to be new and which existing ones can be used), image objectives (for example, ride and performance), and cost estimates.

As it does so, it uncovers the need for tradeoff decisions by NAAO. As this conversion of the concept to detailed form on paper progresses, if it continues to satisfy all Advanced Vehicle Development "clients" (including NAAO, finance, marketing, and the Office of the Chief Executive), the development group produces a prototype. Throughout this process initial pricing judgments are subject to several reviews as both the physical character of the new product takes shape and additional market behavior and cost information becomes available.

Long after final feasibility decisions have been endorsed and final tradeoffs made, earlier pricing judgments may still be modified because of changes in consumer actions or shifts in competitive patterns.

There is no evidence to support the popular belief that in its product planning General Motors (or any of its competitors) uses a uniform "cost plus" formula approach to pricing that is predicated on a targeted rate of return on shareholders' equity. Rather, there is considerable indication that profit margins in terms of both return on sales and return on investment vary considerably from product to product, and that these variances are accepted by the automakers as necessary in their efforts to maintain broad product lines that embrace all mass segments of the market.

One major piece of evidence that would tend to refute the so-called GM pricing formula is the fact that General Motors has not usually achieved the 20 percent rate of return on shareholders' equity that believers in the existence of such a formula regard as its goal. Over the ten-year period from 1968 to 1977 GM's return on equity reached 20 percent in only two years. Its average rate of return on equity for the period was 15.5 percent.

Parochialism

Pricing decisions are not mechanical, and not all parties to them bring similar viewpoints. A typical dichotomy exists between finance and sales groups. The former tends toward pricing decisions that allow somewhat higher margins; the latter typically favors lower prices, primarily in response to the highly volume-oriented dealer organization with which it interacts.

An official of one company interviewed during this study provided an example of the sort of pricing decision which exposes such opposing attitudes. As he explained it, his company was attempting to determine a model-year price for a car line in which almost all important features except one were similar to those of the counterpart product of its principal competitor. That exception—fuel economy—was an area in which his company's product offered the consumer a significant advantage. Finance representatives on the company's pricing committee advocated charging a slight premium for this feature while sales representatives argued that to offer it at no additional cost would provide a more than compensatory, volume-stimulative "edge." "In most cases like this," the official commented, "the salespeople win the argument."

Fine Adjustment Mechanisms

The U.S. automakers set product line prices at the beginning of each model year. These prices are based on the best collective judgments of their executive staffs regarding what price levels will stimulate consumer purchases and maximize the financial return to the company from each product line. By the time such pricing decisions are made, however, most surrounding influences are already fixed. These include the external economy, product costs, consumer reaction to the product (except in the case of a new product line), market share, and competitive behavior. All these virtual "givens" may confront the pricemakers with the need to establish price levels that are likely to generate profitability forecasts which differ greatly from original expectations or from basic corporate objectives.

If consumer response does not match original expectations, an extensive hierarchy of price-related actions can be triggered in an attempt to stimulate increased buying levels. In effect, the auto company can work its way down the hierarchy, making one small adjustment after another until it either achieves the desired result or becomes convinced that pricing action is not the likely route to success. In fact, the first action in the hierarchy is one that occurs without any intervention by the manufacturer and without any direct cost to him. Only midway down the hierarchy is the pricing mechanism fully engaged, as indicated:

1. Dealers, finding themselves with excessive inventory levels of the product line, begin reducing their own profit margins in order to reduce the floor-plan interest costs supporting that inventory.
2. The manufacturer increases the advertising schedule for the product line.
3. The manufacturer launches a contest or some other form of sales incentive program for dealer salespeople and sales managers.
4. The manufacturer undertakes a special promotion aimed at the public, typically offering the product with a specified "package" of popular accessories at a substantial saving from the normal retail price of those accessories; or the manufacturer adjusts the content of the product (by adding a new option) to make it more attractive.
5. The manufacturer provides the dealer with a rebate on dealer inventories of the product line with the expectation that this will be passed through to the public and create a selling momentum.
6. The manufacturer offers fleet discount programs to volume buyers or, more infrequently, offers retail customers a price reduction through the dealers.

Ultimately, the manufacturer, if faced with no other alternative, may offer sizable rebates directly to the public, as was done with selected models in 1975. This, however, was an extreme measure that had no postwar precedent.

6 Price Leadership

The Leadership Role

In any highly concentrated industry the company with the leading position in a particular product/market segment tends to attract its competitors toward its own pricing position. In most (although certainly not all) segments of the U.S. automobile market, General Motors occupies this leadership position. Despite GM's sensitivity to assertions that it is the price leader in those segments where it exercises market leadership, its competitors view this as a basic reality of the business. They consider it an equally basic reality that GM is forced to follow the price leadership of others in those segments, for example, subcompacts, where its position is a secondary one.

General Motors asserts that there is no such thing as a GM pricing position for an entire segment as broad as, for example, standard-sized cars. It also states that although each division's pricing policy has to have company management approval, there is no top-down administration of division pricing. The company also asserts that its divisions compete as energetically against one another through their own dealer organizations as they do against external competition. Naturally, it would be difficult to verify these comments.

Since at least the 1939 investigations of the automobile industry by the Federal Trade Commission, the industry—and General Motors in particular—has been under virtually continual antitrust scrutiny. Observers of the auto industry have contended that antitrust concerns place pressure on GM to avoid seemingly predatory pricing in any market segment, whether the company's position is a leading or a secondary one. At the opposite extreme it is contended that GM must avoid the semblance of "umbrella" pricing (that is, setting price levels high enough to ensure the profitability of competitors) since this might generate such high GM profit levels that they would be viewed as de facto evidence of monopolistic power. General Motors, itself, asserts that neither of these pressures intrudes on its pricing decisions.

Price Leadership Case Histories

Three fairly recent case histories illustrate the responses of different manufacturers to price leadership.

1. *Toyota, Nissan, and Volkswagen, circa 1970.* When Toyota and Nissan made their first strong attempts to create a position in the U.S. market, the

Volkswagen Beetle accounted for 46.0 percent of all imported cars and 6.8 percent of that entire market. At that time the Beetle exemplified the small, economical, high-value automobile. Recognizing the solidness of the Beetle's position and the fact that they had no reputation in the market, Toyota and Nissan chose to establish prices for their leading models nearly 10 percent below that of the most popular VW model. This action, complemented by the quality of their products, enabled these manufacturers to begin making major gains.

2. *The Chevette versus the Corolla and the B210.* When the Chevrolet Division of General Motors introduced its Chevette in 1975, it recognized the dominance of the leading Japanese nameplates in the economy car market. Consequently, it established Chevette's base price at roughly the same level as those of Corolla and the B210. However, despite the strength of the Chevrolet distribution organization, Chevette volume reached only 137,000 units in the first full year and almost certainly generated sizable losses. In reality, GM had priced Chevette well above the segment leaders even though the standard version did not include equipment provided as standard in either the Corolla or the B210.

To help Chevette achieve volume levels that would probably diminish its financial losses and perhaps generate some profit, GM matched the standard equipment offerings of the segment leaders without augmenting Chevette prices. At the beginning of the 1978-model year GM also set a lower price for the Chevette in California (the nation's largest automotive market and the one in which economy imports have achieved the largest market shares) than in other parts of the country.

By spring, Chevette volume, on an annualized basis, reached approximately 230,000 units. General Motors was able to increase Chevette prices four times from January to June as the Japanese automakers increased their prices in response to depreciation of the dollar against the yen.

3. *Introductory pricing of the Omni/Horizon.* In mechanical character and physical configuration the Omni/Horizon resembles the VW Rabbit and the Ford Fiesta more strongly than the Chevette. With a base sticker price differential of approximately $500 between these two imported vehicles and Chevette, Chrysler Corporation had the choice of pricing Omni/Horizon at either extreme or at some point between them. Chrysler concluded that because the Omni/Horizon would be seen in the marketplace primarily as a domestic subcompact car, it had to be priced at the Chevette level (Chevette was the leader in this category). It did this despite the fact that the direct cost of producing the Omni/Horizon is higher than that of producing the Chevette; also, it created a situation where the Omni/Horizon is not likely to prove profitable on a fully allocated cost basis even at high levels of capacity utilization. (This situation has surely been ameliorated, however, by Chrysler's ability to follow GM's Chevette price increases during the first half of the 1978-model year.)

7 Mix and Pricing Policy

Defining *Mix*

Mix can be viewed in two dimensions: vehicle size and upgrading. The size dimension is usually characterized in terms of subcompact, compact, intermediate, and standard. No comparable nomenclature exists for the upgrading dimension, but the auto industry frequently uses the terms *downscale* and *upscale*. Downscale versions of any particular-size car are often also called *base* cars. They are the lowest priced versions offered by a manufacturer in a particular size range and are typically bought with few types of optional equipment. Upscale versions have added styling and comfort features. Consumers typically choose to buy them and load them with a considerable amount of optional equipment.

In terms of general past experience, there has been a pronounced tendency for the sale of subcompact and compact cars to tilt downscale and for intermediate and especially standard cars to tilt upscale.

Significance of Mix

Two major factors underscore the financial importance of mix to the U.S. automakers:

1. *Pricing up from the base car.* It has been traditional in the U.S. automobile business for the base car in any product line to be priced so that it yields very little profit. The base car—particularly in the smaller size ranges but perhaps in larger ranges as well—may be a "loss leader." In other words, on a fully allocated cost basis it may produce a loss. Nonetheless, from a strategic standpoint this pricing policy can be justified in three ways.

First, it creates a price to be used in national advertising that is likely to attract traffic to the dealer showroom and provide dealers with an opportunity to try to sell up. Second, it brings buyers who choose to purchase the base car into the manufacturer's "family." Given the relatively high propensity of new-car buyers to make repeat purchases from the same manufacturer's product line, any loss can be viewed as a short-term investment that is likely to generate a flow of future profits from the expected sale of more upscale products to a satisfied buyer. Third, it contributes additional unit volume, thus helping to push overall production levels for each product line above the critical break-even point into profitable volume ranges.

Typically, styling upgradings of base cars generate substantial incremental profits on the incremental costs required. Typically, too, optional equipment carries a higher margin of profit than the car itself, even when the car is one of the upscale versions of an intermediate- or standard-sized vehicle.

2. *The impact of mix on corporate profits.* In examining the influence of mix on profitability, some basic generalizations can be made which illuminate the subject. First, small-format, U.S.-made cars (subcompacts and compacts) have not generally been as profitable as larger cars in terms of returns on sales. There are several reasons for this:

The labor content of a small, low-priced car is not much lower than that of a larger, higher-priced one, and U.S. labor costs, when viewed internationally, remain relatively high.

The price leadership in the market is in the hands of the importers.

Foreign automakers can amortize tooling over a larger production volume since both their domestic and their export markets are heavily small-car-oriented. Many observers feel that in a mass-market car, a manufacturer would have to produce at least 250,000 units to approach—and around 500,000 units to attain—full economies of scale. In 1977 no U.S. manufacturer made as many as 200,000 of any subcompact configuration. By contrast, we estimate that Toyota produced (for domestic sale and export) 450,000 to 500,000 Corollas, and that Nissan produced between 300,000 and 400,000 B210s.

Although the U.S. manufacturers have offered small cars in styling upgraded versions (the Futura version of Ford Fairmont is an example), in the past the market has not shown as strong a tendency to select these as the more basic versions. Similarly, as reflected in table 7-1, much smaller proportions of buyers choose to equip these cars with profit-generating optional equipment.

Second, larger-format, U.S.-made cars (intermediates and standards) have been more profitable because of the greater market acceptance of the upstyled versions and the higher installation rates of optional equipment.

Consequently, the firm with the greatest relative strength in the larger-format cars (all other things such as direct manufacturing cost and utilization of capacity per major component and per product line being roughly equal) is likely to be the more profitable. This correlates with actual events. During the past four years more than 70 percent of GM's production has typically been in the intermediate- and standard-size ranges. During this same period no more than 47 percent of Chrysler's U.S. production has been in these size ranges, and in 1976 the percentage dropped to 32. Ford's position falls between the two.

Table 7-1

Purchases of Optional Equipment on Selected 1977 New Cars

	Percentage of Total Model Equipped with:				
	Tape Players	*Vinyl Tops*	*Adjustable Steering Wheels*	*Automatic Transmission*	*Air Conditioning*
Subcompact Size					
Ford Pinto	2.4	6.5	NA	61.7	29.5
Chevrolet Monza	3.0	9.0	18.0	68.0	42.0
Upscale Intermediate Size					
Ford Thunderbird/Elite	25.3	89.6	44.5	100.0	95.4
Chevrolet Monte Carlo	12.0	55.0	55.0	100.0	95.0
Standard Size					
Ford	8.5	59.7	28.1	100.0	95.0
Chevrolet	8.0	29.0	45.0	100.0	93.0

Source: *1978 Automotive News Annual* (Detroit: Crain Automotive Group, Inc.), pp. 85-86.

Mix and the Foreign Manufacturers

There seems to be little evidence that such offshore manufacturers as Volkswagen, Toyota, Nissan, and Honda have created for themselves the same sort of mix-related pricing structures that characterize the U.S. manufacturers. There seem to be two reasons for this. First, because all these automakers grew around one or a very few small, utilitarian models, if they could not sell these at a satisfactory profit in their home and export markets, they could not survive as growing corporate entities. Second, rather than depending on the profit impact of upgrading, especially through the incremental profitability of optional equipment, they not only did not expect a large demand for options but also tended to include many items as standard in their base car that U.S. manufacturers typically offered as options.

This pattern, however, may be changing. The two largest Japanese firms, in particular, with their strong growth orientation, their tendency to view General Motors as a model, and the severe growth constraints they face in both Japan and the United States, may be drawn toward a pricing approach more similar to that which has evolved in the United States.

In the past, a strong orientation to growth was an important aspect of the corporate culture of Japanese industry in general. The Japanese automakers were prime examples of this growth orientation, but now a changing domestic and international business environment is forcing these companies to adjust. Some key features of this change are:

1. A maturing home market with only small secular growth rates expected
2. Pressure from the government [the Ministry of International Trade and Industry (MITI)] to stabilize unit volume exported to the United States
3. Strong pressures from appreciation of the yen, forcing the Japanese to raise prices and denying them the lowest priced segment of the U.S. market
4. Cost increases in Japan, especially in wages for the industry's "aging" labor force

The only relief from these pressures is to move toward more luxurious, upscale products with higher-profit-margin potentials.

8 Cost Pressures

A Ring of Pressures

The U.S. automakers face their pricing decisions today in a historic context that was shaped not in the postwar period but even earlier. Further, they see a relatively narrow band each year characterizing the amount that consumers are likely to spend on new automobiles. (Its upper limit is 4.5 percent of PCI.) They also see an overall pricing structure that has proved satisfactory to them as well as to their dealers. Within this structure they recognize the critical importance to their own profitability of a desirable mix.

In addition, the U.S. automakers have experienced a well-defined secular downtrend in the margins they have been able to achieve (that is, ROS levels) since the mid-1960s (see table 8-1). This has been the result of a cost-price pincer, one arm of which has been the conviction of the automakers regarding the pace of price increases that consumers will readily accept without resistance. This has resulted in auto price increases which trail cost-of-living indices. The other arm has been their own costs, which contain some unusual incremental elements.

1. *Labor expense.* The pattern-making collective bargaining agreement reached with the UAW in 1948 established an uncapped cost-of-living adjustment (COLA) that ties wage rates to changes in the cost of living. In addition to this, each three-year renegotiation of contract typically brings with it basic increases in wage levels. Finally, the terms governing company contributions to employee medical expense are open-ended and have been increasing at such a rapid pace that Ford estimates they now account for 12 percent of total compensation, up from 3 percent a decade ago.

2. *Phantom productivity.* The 1948 contracts with the UAW introduced the concept of an "improvement factor" which was viewed as giving the unionized workforce a stake in productivity improvements. This factor, applied to wages, was the annual percentage increase during the prior contract period in overall U.S. manufacturing productivity as measured by the Department of Labor (DoL). Since 1976 the auto workers have received a 3 percent improvement factor; in 1976 it was separated from the DoL productivity index. During the early years of the improvement factor, it is quite likely that auto industry productivity increased more rapidly than that of general industry. However, during the last decade its increments may be well below 3 percent, in part because of the difficulty of finding enough affordable means of improving the production process and in part because of the workforce itself.

Table 8-1
Five-Year Rolling Averages of Net Return on Sales—General Motors,
Ford, and Chrysler, 1958-1977

Last Year of Five-Year Period	GM	Ford	Chrysler
1958	8.0	4.6	1.3
1959	7.9	4.9	1.1
1960	7.5	4.8	0.7
1961	7.5	5.1	0.6
1962	8.0	5.5	0.5
1963	8.6	*6.1*	1.7
1964	9.0	5.8	2.8
1965	9.6	5.8	3.5
1966	*9.8*	5.6	4.0
1967	9.4	4.5	*4.8*
1968	9.0	4.3	4.1
1969	8.4	4.0	3.3
1970	7.0	3.5	2.4
1971	6.5	3.3	2.0
1972	6.3	4.0	1.8
1973	6.2	3.9	1.4
1974	5.4	3.4	1.0
1975	5.4	3.0	0.6
1976	5.3	2.9	0.9
1977	5.1	3.0	0.6

Source: Corporate annual reports, 1959-1978.
Note: Italic numbers represent peak figures.

3. *Suprainflationary inputs.* Especially since 1974 some of the inputs to the production process (most notably energy itself, petrochemicals, and energy-intensive raw materials) have increased in price much more rapidly than the general rates of inflation. Based on the input-output tables for the U.S. economy, these sorts of inputs probably account for nearly one-third of total cost.

4. *New costs.* The combination of the sharp upturn in direct product liability and recall expense, layered on top of additional design and manufacturing efforts to minimize both, has added a new and wholly incremental cost element.

5. *Regulatory add-ons.* As noted earlier, federal requirements since 1968 have added appreciably to the cost of an average new car.

Responses to the Pressures

The automakers, in the face of a situation which they believe has led them to price their products at levels which have yielded progressively shrinking margins, have responded in two major ways, one quite visible and the other much less so.

1. *Resistance to costly regulatory add-ons.* Aside from considerations of technical merit, they have struggled against the imposition of such hardware systems as the air bag because it will add a substantial cost increment without, they believe, any counterbalancing consumer perception of incremental value.

2. *Relative decline in new investment.* Shrinking unit profits on only modestly growing unit sales levels can generate traditional levels of return on investment only if the investment base itself increases at a much lower rate. Despite the massiveness of the automakers' overall dollar expenditures on new plant and tooling, they have—until very recently—been spending *relatively* less on capital investment than they did in the early 1960s. (Table 8-2 illustrates this sort of trend at General Motors.) They have been setting higher target rates of return[1] for new investment projects and have been using standardization, of both mechanical and body components, as a means of doing this.

Note

1. Target rates of return, or "hurdle rates," are the minimum rates applied by a corporation to proposals for discretionary investment projects. When incremental investment capital is scarce (for example, in periods of prolonged low profitability or limited availability and high cost of borrowed funds), such rates may be raised to higher levels. This stems from the natural desire of the corporate entity to channel all the investments it has the resources to make into those projects with the most favorable financial prospects.

Table 8-2
General Motors—Total Investment as Percentage of Total Revenues, 1968-1977

1968	9.3%
1969	8.9%
1970	9.3%
1971	8.4%
1972	7.8%
1973	7.5%
1974	7.5%
1975	6.3%
1976	6.2%
1977	6.3%

Source: GM annual reports.

Note: These are five-year rolling averages with each year representing the last year of the series. Therefore, the percentage given for 1968 is an average of the percentages for 1964, 1965, 1966, 1967, and 1968.

9 Future Concerns and Future Actions

Concerns

The current set of regulatory requirements confronts the automakers with two types of financially related changes and challenges.

1. *Organic change.* In the down-sizing and redesign of entire vehicle families to meet corporate average fuel economy standards, the principal financially related change is the large amount of capital investment required in a relatively brief period. Therefore, circumstances prevent the automakers from continuing their decade-long policy of reducing the relative role of capital investment as a means of buoying up ROI.

2. *Add-on change.* To comply with current passenger safety and emissions control standards, new hardware will have to be added to each vehicle. This will have a wholly incremental impact on direct cost.

Even though both forms of change may generate consumer benefits, as noted earlier, there is considerable and seemingly reasonable doubt as to whether consumers will perceive these benefits as equivalent to the costs associated with them if the costs are passed through in pricing. Even increased fuel economy, an extremely tangible and direct benefit, is collected by the auto owner only gradually.[1] The automakers feel that consumers may have what amounts to an extremely high mental discount rate on future-related advantages of this sort.

The automakers are likely to find that despite their historic policy of striving to keep price increases gradual and below the level of inflation, the new financial calculus they face leaves them little choice but to pass through such cost increments. This will probably increase prices more rapidly than the rate of inflation. Consumer response, then, becomes the critical factor:

Will consumers, confronting rapidly rising car prices without complementary perceived benefits, stretch out their purchasing patterns much as they do in periods of recession?

Will consumers, rather than delaying new-car purchases, merely downgrade the types of vehicles they buy?

Will consumers do both?

Any of or all these patterns are likely to diminish the internal generation of cash for CAFE-related investment programs and, in particular, exaggerate the financing difficulties of the smaller, financially weaker firms.

Future Actions

The likely actions of the U.S. automakers in the face of this array of concerns will revolve primarily on three areas of management policy, all already quite visible.

1. *Capital conservation.* The firms will do everything possible to limit capital investment. Regulatory-essential projects will be pursued under tight controls. Nonregulatory proposals will be subjected to high hurdle rates, and even some of the most attractive may not be implemented because of a lack of capital. Efforts such as Ford's contract to purchase power train components from Toyo Kogyo and AMC's decision to buy (from Pontiac Division) rather than make four-cylinder engines will be pursued wherever possible.

2. *Standardization.* The trend toward progressively less differentiation from nameplate to nameplate in a single manufacturer's product line will not only continue but will probably increase. This will be the primary mechanism for restraining the impact of tooling, manufacturing, and materials management costs.

3. *Pass-through pricing.* There will be an inevitable tendency to pass through regulatory cost increases despite automaker concerns about possible adverse consumer behavior. More than likely, this will be done in ways that soften the visibility of such actions (for example, by reducing the array of standard equipment in selected or all models as a cost offset) or by testing their impact through frequent, relatively small price changes. (This latter approach may have only limited potential because of its impact on vendor relations. Typically, vendors are given the opportunity of raising their own prices only once a year. They may press for more frequent price changes if the automakers, themselves, persist in doing so.)

Note

1. Savings on gasoline expenditures would average $65 a year for the 1978-1981 period and $75 a year for the 1980-1983 period (the interval in which CAFE requirements will increase most). These calculations were made using three-year segments to best reflect the typical new-car buying cycle. They are based on assumptions of an average of 10,000 miles being driven per year and gasoline being priced at $0.65 per gallon.

Part III
Manufacturers and the
Marketplace

The National Highway Traffic Safety Administration has asked Harbridge House to comment on the ways in which automakers endeavor to shape the market for their products and the ways in which they react to shifts in that market. In particular, we were asked to address four questions:

1. To what extent are manufacturers able to influence the marketplace, in both the long and the short term, through marketing strategies?
2. What means are available to them to alter, both slightly and drastically, demand in the marketplace?
3. What strategies do they undertake, given long product planning lead times, to ensure that their product mixes satisfy future market demand? Once the process is underway, what adjustments can be made?
4. How are they able to influence market demand during a model year through various available marketing techniques?

In the background, however, NHTSA expressed a question of even greater interest: What is the potential capability of the automakers to shift market demand toward safer and/or more fuel-efficient vehicles?

A reading of part IV illuminates many of these questions. Therefore, in this intentionally brief part III we will draw on our research, both that focused explicitly on the decision-making process and that of a more general nature, to present some broad summary answers to the questions listed.

10 Character of the Market and Automaker Adaptation to It

No market that can account for as much as $50 billion in retail sales annually is likely to lend itself to characterization by simple generalization. The forces that shape any aspect of so large and so segmented a market are typically complex. They involve an interplay between the economy as a whole, the attitudes of consumers, the initiatives of manufacturers, the behavior of franchised dealers, and a multiplicity of surrounding forces and "players." Among the latter, government has clearly moved from playing a minor role to a center-stage position. Therefore, in briefly commenting on some key aspects of the market, we would not suggest that we are attempting to enumerate every influence on each aspect and on interrelationships; instead, we are focusing only on what appear to be some of the predominant ones.

Secular Demand

For the past twenty-five years new-car unit sales have continued to increase at a fairly consistent rate of approximately 3 percent per annum. Annual unit sales, of course, fluctuate widely but seldom outside a range of plus or minus 10 percent of the long-term trend line.

During the past decade, basic indicators of vehicle ownership have largely stabilized, as demonstrated by the following statistics:

Households owning one or more automobiles reached 80 percent of all households in 1971 and appear to have held at a point just slightly above that percentage.

Households owning two or more cars continued increasing as a percentage of total households until 1973 when they peaked at 28.4 percent. The percentage dropped 1.5 points in the wake of the 1973 oil crisis.

The size of the market and its growth rate seem to be primarily the result of annual shifts in the economy, consumer affluence and attitudes, and demographics and residential dispersion of the population. The influence exerted by the automakers appears to be largely that of attempting to optimize opportunities for the industry that are embedded in these broader trends. A major strategic theme in this optimization, perhaps *the* major one, has been the sort of relative stability of pricing described in part II.

Mass-Market Orientation

The essential design/production strategy of the Big Three over the past decade has been to generate a shrinking number of basic vehicle configurations and to broaden the appeal of each one by offering a wide variety of bodies, trim combinations, power trains, and option packages. This enables each automaker to offer individualized products in different segments and subsegments of the overall market while personally benefiting from economies of production scale and economies of standardization.

The resulting diversity of products is segmented symbolically. Not only do the automakers use their advertising to report to consumers that they have what the consumer appears to be seeking (as revealed in past buying patterns and future-oriented research) but they also link each product group with symbols to which potential buyers are likely to respond. During the 1950s the automotive industry and its advertising agencies were prime consumers of motivational research, a concept originated by Dr. Ernest Dichter, who asserted that it could uncover the strong unconscious buying motives which were the primary influences on buyer behavior. Some of the enthusiasm for such elaborate, quasi-Freudian methods of profiling consumer motives diminished when the Edsel, whose design was said to be strongly influenced by such research, failed so disastrously.

The automakers do not, however, attempt to satisfy all segments and subsegments. For example, they dropped convertible bodies from their product offerings when demand levels no longer supported economical production of these models. As for imported subcompact cars, these were not challenged until they captured more than 10 percent of the market because the size of the market segment and the potential unit profit, even at efficient production volume levels, did not produce an attractive enough financial prospect to merit the investment. In the opinion of Detroit, imports, and the great diversity of appeals they generate, reflect much of the nonmass elements of the market, the residue that the Big Three believe they cannot reach economically.

**Creativity of the Marketplace
and of the Automakers**

It appears that consumers themselves may be the primary innovators of new types of vehicles while the automakers are the primary innovators of comfort, convenience, and performance features. This apparent paradox is rooted in the relatively high cost and risk that a manufacturer faces today in launching an innovative vehicle type. Therefore, manufacturers will not typically invest in a novel vehicle format unless there is evidence of consumer readiness to accept the concept. Examples from the past and present are plentiful:

1. *Station wagons.* These were not launched as a vehicle type until such wagons had been improvised from light truck chassis and configurations.
2. *Muscle cars.* Through modification of standard showroom vehicles, enthusiasts of the NASCAR type of racing began to approximate the stock car racers. The extent of this activity indicated a base of interest in high-performance cars.
3. *Vans.* The rise in van sales and the customization of these vehicles currently seem to be leading the automakers toward the production of factory "customized" vans and probably toward new-product programs in this segment.

Until the introduction of stringent federal rule making in fuel consumption, occupant safety, and emissions control, much of the innovative effort undertaken by the automakers was focused on incrementality, that is, comfort, performance, and convenience features that tended to increase the price of the consumer purchase and increase more than proportionally the profitability of that purchase to the dealer and manufacturer. Typical examples are automatic transmissions, air conditioning, electrical seat and window controls, and engine and carburetion options.

Macro Inertia and Micro Responsiveness

Some aspects of the passenger car market have shown remarkable stability. For example,

> *New-car retention.* Throughout the past twenty-five years new-car buyers, on average, have retained their cars for three years. This pattern continued even as the average length of purchase financing increased sharply in 1974.

> *Brand buyer profiles.* Even though the real distinctions between vehicles offered under different nameplates of the same manufacturer have diminished to a largely cosmetic degree, distinctions between buyer populations continue to reflect price and product differences of twenty or more years ago.

Other aspects, however, have proved to be extremely volatile. In 1973, for example, nearly 40 percent of all new cars purchased were of standard size; by 1977 standard-sized cars accounted for less than 25 percent of all new cars purchased. Shifts of even greater magnitude may occur year to year in the popularity of individual models. For example, through June 20 of the current year, sales of the Aspen/Volare declined 30 percent; the new A-body Oldsmobile Cutlass was selling at only 60 percent the rate of its predecessor; and sales of

Mustang II, a model in its last year, were 19 percent above prior-year sales. This potential for rapid shifts, sometimes influenced by competitive behavior (as appears to be the case to a great extent in the Aspen/Volare situation) and sometimes by unreceptiveness of consumers to new models (as in the instance of Cutlass), occupies much of the marketing attention and resources of the manufacturers.

11 Intent of Market-Related Planning

United States automobile manufacturers have come to expect that swings in the consumer economy, even in monthly payment terms by two out of three buyers, will have a more than proportionate effect on their respective businesses. As producers of high-priced consumer durables, they also know that consumers can easily postpone buying decisions in the short term but not in the longer run. Year-to-year sorts of shifts are a matter of course for the auto industry, and, in fact, the automobile production system, with its extensive use of overtime as a capacity extender, has been shaped around them. Although the automakers employ a considerable number and variety of tactical marketing tools to mitigate the effect of cyclical downturns, their market-related planning tends to focus more on a view of the market in which annual "kinks" are flattened out into more secular trend patterns.

The Market View as It Figures in Product Planning

From a business financial standpoint, the goal of any automaker's product planning program usually encompasses all or nearly all the following intentions:

1. To retain or gain market share within a product segment (one common view of segmentation is by size: subcompact, compact, intermediate, and standard. Within a particular segment there may be a variety of product subsegments such as luxury, sporty, and station wagon.)
2. To improve product mix overall (that is, to sell a higher proportion of relatively high-profit vehicles such as upscale standard-sized cars and a lower proportion of relatively low-profit vehicles such as downscale compact or subcompact cars)
3. To improve mix within a segment (that is, for example, to sell a high proportion of luxury models in each size segment)
4. To establish a proprietary niche in the market with a product that is perceived by consumers to be sharply different from those offered by the competition

The market, then, becomes a tradeoff between what each manufacturer would like it to be (high volume and a high profit mix) and the ways in which consumers react to the totality of the offerings made by all manufacturers. The results emerging from this interaction often go against the intent of all manufacturers or of individual manufacturers. The relative growth in popularity of intermediate-sized cars at the expense of standard sizes during the past five years illustrates a macro trend of this sort. Another is the sales mix of Chrysler Corporation during the early to mid-1970s, which skewed strongly toward relatively low-profit, downscale compact cars, thereby depressing the corporation's profit potential.

The product planning process is designed to bring together the business goals of a company with the demonstrated or expected preferences of consumers and interweave the two.

The Impact of Time

The new-product development cycle—the time from the commitment to undertake a project to the roll-out of "job 1"—has stretched rapidly in the U.S. automobile industry. In the early 1970s when General Motors made its decision to begin down-sizing its B-body standard-sized vehicles, the cycle was approximately three years; today it appears to fall in the range of six to seven years.

The relatively short cycles that prevailed prior to the establishment of the CAFE formula stemmed from the fact that much of the newness of new products was in styling or in discretionary introductions of technology. Even the initial GM down-sizing programs (both for the B-body and then for the A-body families of vehicles) involved, by current/future standards, relatively straightforward redesign of vehicle configurations and similarly straightforward efforts to "sweat" weight out by a variety of means, among which materials substitution figured prominently. With short product development cycles, business strategies and product concepts benefited in confidence level from a closer-view of the market. (Planners can obviously have much greater confidence in their view of how the market is likely to behave in three years than in seven.)

The lengthening of the planning cycle is primarily attributable to the organic nature of the sorts of changes required to ensure compliance with CAFE standards. In particular, development lead times are notably long for new engines. The varieties of tradeoffs that must be explored grow in both number and complexity. Glass thickness, for example, has remained unvaried for many years; reducing the thickness, however, would save substantial amounts of weight, but what effect would that have on interior noise levels or on occupant safety? And how long might it take to create a new type of glass that could provide current noise barrier and safety features in thinner gauges? The combination of organic newness, novel technology, and the complementary need to introduce redesigned components that must be thoroughly tested all force a backing up of start dates. With this comes a progressively lower level of confidence that whatever is being planned will notch well into consumer wishes and needs as much as seven years hence. In addition, investments in new products are of an order of magnitude that major mistakes, instead of being erasable, can themselves erase giant corporations.

An additional impact of both time and the CAFE standards in the product planning process is that some products will be transitional ones needed to help their manufacturers meet the early CAFE requirements but not sufficiently fuel-efficient to help meet the later ones. In other words, "quick fixes" of design technology were used to meet the early standards rather than attempting to force the mix drastically toward the smaller existing product configurations. Consequently, on such transitional products, tooling costs will not be spread over as long a product life cycle as might normally be desirable to a manufacturer.

The only defense for product planners is to shape the planning process so that key decisions from which there is no possibility of retreat are deferred as long as possible. In simpler terms, product planners attempt to keep as many options open as they can and for as long as they can.

At Ford, for instance, the firm's long-term business strategy spawns a product development strategy. One of its main facets is a series of alternative "cycle plans," each of them embodying a different sequencing of new products, extensively modified products, and face-lifted products. Each cycle plan contains, in itself, several alternative courses for arriving at more or less the same end point. As one of the various proposed cycle plans is adopted, its new-product elements are developed conceptually. In other words, the products are described in detail on paper in terms of character, dimensions, weight, performance, price, image, and major components. Once these have been approved, the concept is developed in even greater detail by an advanced vehicle development group that usually prepares a mechanical prototype (that is, an existing car, modified, so it is largely similar to the intended new car) or a style prototype (that is, a handmade replica of the intended new car). Once a new-product prototype is approved, the producing division begins to engineer it for production.

The formalized process attempts to identify key decision points and to withhold decisions until the ultimate possible moment. In practice, this is proving to be difficult because of the technological and tooling lead times required. For example, one manufacturer is still attempting to postpone a decision relating to its 1983-1984 product lines in which the essential choice is between a particular power plant and an additional effort at down-sizing, largely because of the fogginess and instability of the market and the regulatory environment, especially with regard to emissions and consumer behavior respecting smaller vehicle configurations. But such decisions cannot be held off much longer.

Essentially, more and more point-of-no-return decisions are being made with progressively less reliable market information. Even a decision to produce a sporty body for a new basic car configuration must now be made two to two-and-one-half years before introduction. Naturally this is a source of unease for the auto companies as well as one of the principal reasons for their repeatedly voiced concerns regarding consumer acceptance of new-car configurations designed to meet fuel economy standards.

12 Implementation of Marketing Efforts

The constraints under which automaker marketing groups, programs, and resources are deployed are significant and worth enumerating:

1. Unlike the situation in other consumer product fields, including many consumer durables, automakers have little ability to influence the physical character of their products quickly in response to consumer reactions.

2. The unique distribution system in the auto industry permits some employment of "push" marketing, but, because of the importance to manufacturers of the financial well-being of their franchised dealers, it can be utilized to only a limited degree.

3. Marketplace resistance to the product/market programs and goals of the automakers often tends to be reflected in forces so powerful that they are not readily susceptible to any considerable influence of marketing efforts. Examples include economic downturns or expectations of them; strong negative reactions to a new model; or, as in 1974, concerns regarding the future availability of gasoline.

Operating within these constraints, marketing efforts focused on the short to medium term have often achieved impressive results. Typically, the outcome seems to depend primarily on a combination of the difficulty of the undertaking involved and the extent of the resources employed.

Marketing Tools

The principal short-term marketing tools available to the automakers are advertising, price, and dealer promotion. Frequently, as outlined in part II, promotional campaigns conducted at the dealer level may themselves be essentially price-based since they involve price concessions to dealers which the dealers then have the option of passing through to customers or of converting to some mix of higher commissions to their sales force and higher gross margins to themselves.

The automakers are among the largest national advertisers. However, the percentage of revenues they budget for media advertising is well below 1 percent, considerably beneath the percentage typically spent by manufacturers of most consumer nondurable products. There are considerable economies of scale in advertising so that the largest companies, General Motors and Ford, commonly spend smaller percentages of their revenues on advertising and smaller amounts per unit sold than their competitors.

The automakers' own national campaigns are supplemented by the advertising programs of regional dealer associations. The aggregate of the regional dealer advertising programs virtually doubles the advertising effort of each manufacturer.

The orchestration of marketing efforts to contend with a short- to medium-term issue generally begins with activities initiated by individual dealers and escalates through a series of advertising, promotional, and pricing steps like those discussed in part II.

Effectiveness of Short-Term Efforts

Two recent and successful efforts of the Chevrolet Division of General Motors illustrates the deployment of marketing resources to deal with short- to medium-term problems.

1. *Chevette.* Sales of GM's U.S. adaptation of the Opel Kadet reached only about 170,000 units during the vehicle's first fifteen months in the market. Assuming the typically low profitability level attached to U.S. small-car programs even at efficient production volumes, Chevette must have been generating substantial losses since its sales levels did not permit normal production efficiency. In the 1978-model year GM lowered the Chevette sticker price nationally, lowered it further in California (the state with the highest penetration by imported cars), and included as standard equipment a wide variety of items formerly listed as extra-cost options. Chevette sales for the first six months of calendar year 1978 reached 124,000 units, and Chevrolet has since announced plans to open a second Chevette assembly line. It is likely that the combination of sales volumes which permit efficient production and price increases facilitated by yen/dollar-related increases by the Japanese manufacturers have made Chevette into at least a modestly profitable program for Chevrolet.

2. *Malibu.* When initial months' sales of the down-sized 1978 Chevrolet intermediate, the Malibu, fell below those of its predecessor, Chevrolet evidently increased its national advertising budget for the Malibu and, by December, had turned the situation around so that 1978-model sales in that month exceeded those of the 1977 model. By June, sales of the new Malibu surpassed those of the old by 50 percent.

Recently, an executive from American Motors speculated that had General Motors been confronted with the same sorts of problems AMC faced with the Pacer, GM could have made the Pacer into a success. He felt that GM could have invested enough in advertising for the Pacer (as it did with the 1978 Malibu) to make the public feel more comfortable and familiar with the car's novel profile and that the strong GM "pipeline" (its own regional sales organizations and dealer groups) would have persisted in pressing the Pacer concept on the public.

13 Toward Federal Goals

In approaching the question of the ability of the automakers, through their marketing capability, to shift demand toward safer and/or more fuel-efficient vehicles, it is necessary to first look at the automakers' own business orientation and at the existing consumer safety/fuel attitudes that influence demand.

Automakers' business orientation. The culture of any sort of business entity in any industry would condition its managers to assess any proposed change in their business through the same set of criteria. In the auto industry we believe these criteria are (1) improvement in market share, (2) improvement in overall mix, (3) improvement in mix within a segment, and (4) establishment of a proprietary niche.

Existing consumer attitudes. To what extent are consumer attitudes receptive to product and marketing initiatives taken by one or more automakers in regard to safety and fuel efficiency? Does potential receptivity lead to the belief that an automaker's efforts to target on a particular initiative would strike a responsive chord?

Consumer Attitudes

During the past several years *Newsweek* magazine has commissioned a series of annual market studies of new-car buyers that have been conducted by Beta Research Corporation of Syosset, New York. Findings generated in the 1973, 1974, and 1977 studies are particularly revealing.

Safety

Of the 1973 buyer population responding to the question, 80 percent either definitely favored additional safety devices or indicated that it might favor them. However, slightly more than half of those responding indicated an unwillingness to pay any extra for such additional safety devices. In 1974 Beta focused specifically on air bags. Slightly more than 40 percent of those responding indicated they either would or might favor air bags at additional cost; the median price they expressed a willingness to pay was in the $50 to $74 range. In the 1977 buyer study only 17 percent of those responding considered air bags or other passive restraints as essential safety features in a new car, a frequency of mention far behind impact-absorbing bumpers, safety belts, better braking systems, better tires, improved rear stoplight and signal systems, and even more powerful headlights.

These sorts of attitudes plus low actual seat belt use, little support for mandatory seat belt use laws (only half of the *Newsweek* interviewees responding indicated they would or might favor such legislation), and the lack of mention of safety as a major buying motive reflect a seemingly modest level of consumer interest in safety.

Fuel Economy

In the summer of 1974, with the oil embargo and gasoline price increases fresh in people's consciousness, 59 percent of the people interviewed by Beta Research felt that the automakers should make smaller cars and 77 percent felt that they should cut horsepower; however, only 23 percent indicated that they would be likely to buy a smaller car if gas prices continued to increase or if gasoline were in short supply. Nonetheless, nearly one-third of the 1974 new-car buyers indicated that economy, mostly fuel economy, was their principal motive for buying a new car, and this was the second most frequently mentioned motive. By the 1977 buyer study, the general economy and fuel economy had declined in relative importance among buyers of domestic cars to about half that of the 1974 group; however, these held about the same importance in 1977 as in 1974 for buyers of imported cars.

Automaker Attitudes

The sorts of consumer attitudes enumerated almost certainly have been explored by the U.S. automakers in their own consumer research. They reflect only slight receptivity to product/marketing initiatives in the safety area. Given the sorts of criteria against which automakers would be expected to assess product/ marketing initiatives, safety would thus not appear to be likely to figure importantly.

Some bits of experience would appear to reinforce this assessment. For example, in 1956 the Ford Division launched a safety-oriented marketing program. In that same year Chevrolet gained 2 percentage points of market share advantage over Ford. Volvo, alone among passenger car marketers in the United States, has stressed safety strongly in its advertising. The appeal of this safety orientation has not prevented Volvo sales from sinking and remaining well below the peak levels achieved in 1973-1975.

Fuel economy, however, has assumed two new dimensions in the product/ marketing priorities of U.S. automakers:

Under the CAFE concept all the automakers must sell substantial numbers of small, highly fuel-efficient (and, at least in the past, relatively low-profit) vehicles so that they can also sell substantial numbers of bigger, less fuel-efficient (and more profitable), luxurious cars. To compete against imports and against one another in this segment of the market, comparative fuel economy is a "hard number" that can be used to point to competitive advantage.

Consciousness of fuel economy exists even among buyers for whom it is not a major motive. This consciousness and the specificity that ratings assigned by the Environmental Protection Agency provide have encouraged the automakers to at least include fuel economy among their selling arguments.

It is unlikely, however, that fuel economy will climb in importance as a marketing factor unless gasoline prices jump radically or fuel supply is substantially diminished. From 1975 through the first half of 1978, a period characterized by gradually increasing gas prices but adequate fuel supplies, the standard and intermediate segments of the new-car market remained relatively stable. However, if consumer purchasing behavior were to become strongly skewed toward the larger, less fuel-efficient vehicles, the auto manufacturers would have to act to influence large numbers of buyers to purchase smaller, more fuel-efficient vehicles in order to ensure compliance with CAFE requirements.

Part IV
The Decision-Making
Process

The single most significant factor about the decision-making process used by the major automakers is the extent to which it has been pressured by recent externalities. These pressures have not always changed the decision-making "cultures" of each company, but they have tested them severely, forced them to generate modifications in organizational philosophy, and at times surfaced their individual weaknesses. The magnitude of the externalities is forcing the major automakers to change their pace of decision making (and implementing) from a walk to double time. The two externalities that have been most influential are:

1. *Federal regulation.* The influence of federal regulation has been felt primarily by U.S. automobile manufacturers because it involves rapid acceleration of new-product development and introduction. Because of the nonproportionality of investment needs, it threatens to further concentrate market strength and to alter the relative financial strengths of the companies.
2. *Real or potential loss of market share because of currency relationships and/or U.S. protectionism.* The influence here was first felt by Volkswagen but is currently placing an increasing hold on the thinking of the Japanese automakers. Natural tendencies to hope that the problem will dissipate are reinforced by concerns regarding the effects on employment in the home country if majors manufacturing programs are launched in the United States.

The shifting of gears in decision making into this new range has not been entirely smooth for all the auto companies, as is discussed. Some of the principal features of the decision-making process used by the automakers and some of the major differences in the process from company to company are highlighted.

Personalized versus Institutionalized
Decision Making

In General Motors and in the Japanese companies, the strategic decisionmaking process has been intentionally depersonalized. Each has a culture based on consensus. General Motors' has been imposed through a creative effort led by Alfred P. Sloan, Jr., and based on both the interlocking committee structure and a body of managers who have spent their entire careers in the company. Although the "system" in the Japanese firms is rooted in the national culture

117

and lacks many of the explicit organizational manifestations implanted by Sloan at GM, it does not appear to differ greatly in philosophy or operation.

At Ford, Chrysler, and American Motors, despite the presence of some types of formalized strategic planning, strategic decisions have tended to take on more of a personalized character. Evidence of this is the ability to trace major strategic thrusts to individuals. At Chrysler, partly because of its size, its financial situation, and the current managerial transition, there is a growing tendency to broaden the number of senior managers involved in major decisions; nonetheless, it remains a small group.

Volkswagen and Honda appear to be in the midst of a notable shift from personalized to institutionalized decision making. At VW this transition flows from Toni Schmücker's philosophy of how a large company should be managed. At Honda it is occurring primarily as a consequence of the retirement of Soichiro Honda and Takeo Fujisawa, its creators, from active involvement in the firm and their replacement at the helm by a new generation of managers.

The Importance of Relative Size

American Motors recorded sales of $2.24 billion in 1977. Bristol-Myers is of almost exactly the same size. Nonetheless, Bristol-Myers, a leader in its industry, seems a large company and AMC, in its staffing, resources, and outlook, seems a small one. Thus, in the auto industry relative size rather than absolute size is a key factor in automaker decision making.

Chrysler, larger than all but nine other U.S. manufacturing firms, is considerably thinner than its competitors in staff numbers and capability and as thin as financially prosperous firms in other industries where annual revenues may be only 20 percent as large as Chrysler's. Chrysler may be a huge company, but in its own industry it is one of only moderate size and it acts accordingly. Even Ford, the third largest manufacturing enterprise in the United States, frequently "poor-mouths" when its executives speak of their options, opportunities, and resources.

This same sort of relativity exists in the Japanese auto industry to some degree, but its character differs. Nissan is a much closer number two to Toyota than Ford is to GM, and Nissan continually strives to close the gap. Nonetheless, the components of that gap are so deeply rooted that Toyota's advantage appears to be growing with time rather than shrinking. Honda would be expected to feel much of the relative disadvantage so frequently expressed at Chrysler, yet the newness of the firm, the dynamic character of its growth, the "differentness" of its products, and the spirit of its management all seem to diminish the constant sense of being a small fish in a pond inhabited by two whales.

The most important impact of relative size on strategic decision making appears to be in the range of alternatives that can be pursued. The larger, financially healthier firms are able to pursue alternatives in their product planning and development that the weaker firms cannot. The latter must instead freeze largely on one strategy, a strategy that has relatively few opportunities for modification as market and competitive patterns emerge and change during the product development cycle. The Pacer was an outcome of this sort of limitation at AMC. Similarly, the relatively smaller companies are forced to do more things "on the cheap." The cosmetic upgrading of Aspen/Volare into a "new" luxury car (Diplomat/LeBaron) exemplifies this situation.

The Relative Absence of Traditional, Formal Long-Range Planning

In most U.S. companies the idea of a rolling five- or seven-year strategic plan, updated annually and fortified by individual plans of major components (sometimes called "strategic planning units") that feed into an overall corporate plan, has been grafted onto managerial systems for at least the last decade. This sort of planning system that generates a tangible "plan" (that is, a document embodying planning assumptions, objectives, strategies, and actions for implementation) is far from a universal process at the eight automakers. Ford, Toyota, and Volkswagen are moving strongly in that direction. General Motors does a great deal of strategic planning but does not appear to generate "a plan." The other firms all utilize some elements of formalized corporate strategic planning but do not seem to create a comprehensive planning document.

It seems that in the auto industry product planning is a much more highly developed, culturally integrated process than strategic planning. The creation of the corporate strategy and analysis group at Ford approximately one year ago is particularly revealing since its charter is not that of overseeing the creation of a traditional plan but rather that of helping the office of the chief executive make better strategic decisions. To some extent this, in itself, is a reflection of the centralization and personalization of major decisions in that company.

Product Planning under Pressure

The product planning process typically begins with an effort to identify consumer interests and to integrate these with such business objectives as profitability, volume growth, and improved market share. This has always been a long process, but its length has grown dramatically in the past five years. The cycle requires at least five years for a new product that does not embody unusual new technology and may require more than seven years if new technology is extensive.

This lengthening of the new-product planning cycle forces planners to make basic decisions without the confidence that a close-in view of market behavior provides. Although product planning systems have been structured to delay "point of no return" decisions as long as possible, these decisions are still being made much farther out than they were a decade ago.

The cost of developing new products which meet both federal regulatory standards and automaker views of consumer needs is so high, compared with any prior experience of the industry, that it is causing significant changes in organizational philosophy within the automotive companies. The most notable change has been the withdrawal of traditional product design autonomy from the various General Motors divisions and the use of the "project center" (in reality a program management office) as the organizational mechanism for centralizing product development under corporate rather than division control.

14 American Motors Corporation

Overview

The smallest and financially most precarious of the U.S. automakers, American Motors in its short history has developed an organizational structure that reflects its relative size and financial condition. Among the company's officers not more than six people appear to be strategic decisionmakers, and much of the decision-making power is concentrated in the president and chairman. The quest for smallness is carried through the AMC staff as well. For example, the whole product planning and development process does not involve more than one hundred people. To compensate for its small staff size, AMC uses outside organizations extensively in such areas as law and marketing.

In a small organization such as AMC the chief executive officer (CEO) is bound to exert a relatively large influence on corporate strategy. Shortly after the founding of the company in 1954 through the merger of Nash-Kelvinator and Hudson, George Romney became its CEO. Chiefly through his influence the new company carved out a strategy independent from that of its Big Three competitors. Romney personally promoted and implemented the concept of the compact car and imbued the organization with his own enthusiasm. He managed to bring the firm to a position where it held 6.5 percent of the market in 1960. The following year he left the firm to become the Governor of Michigan.

The charismatic Romney was succeeded by Roy Abernethy who had a successful career in sales and marketing. Faced with increasing competition from domestic compacts and small imports, Abernethy attempted to increase AMC's volume by selling a broad line of models much like that of the Big Three. Under his direction the company gradually lost its identity and suffered from an eroding market position.

In 1967 Roy D. Chapin, Jr., the son of one of the founders of the Hudson Motor Car Company, took over as chairman and CEO. This marked the beginning of a new era for AMC. Under Chapin the company formulated the "philosophy of difference" that returned it to its original strategy of selling primarily small cars. Chapin was instrumental in the merger between AMC and the money-losing Jeep Corporation in 1970. This merger, considered a mistake by practically everybody in the industry at the time, turned out to be the foundation for AMC's continuing existence.

Also in 1967, William V. Luneburg was appointed president and chief operating officer. Luneburg had a strong background in manufacturing and finance. Aggressive and outspoken, he formed a remarkably close management team with the calm and courtly Chapin, and together they ruled the company for almost a decade. In 1977 Luneburg retired. In the same year Chapin relinquished the CEO function to Gerald C. Meyers, a protege of Luneburg. Meyers had been responsible for the development of most of AMC's product line and took credit for the revamping of the Jeep line. As CEO, Meyers will exert considerable influence in shaping the future direction of AMC. Chapin, if only because of his long tenure in the automobile industry, will continue to play an important role as chairman of the board.

Most of AMC's current organizational structure and policies were put into place by the Chapin-Luneburg management team. The structure is fairly straightforward with staff and line functions reporting to four group vice presidents who, in turn, report to the CEO. Strategic decisions are made primarily in two committees: the policy committee and the product committee. The policy committee includes the chairman, the president, the group vice president for corporate staff, and a representative of the finance function. Key operating and long-range planning decisions are made in this committee. The product committee includes all the policy committee members plus the group vice presidents for operations and for car and Jeep vehicles. This committee formulates AMC's product strategy.

The organizational structure itself, however, gives only a partial picture of AMC's management process. What really makes AMC stand out from its larger competitors is the degree of informality with which decisions are made within the company. This informality is a direct result of AMC's remarkably lean executive-level staff who, because of their few numbers, are practically in continuous informal contact with one another. As Roy Chapin once stated, "AMC's decision-making process is not a lot different from General Motors', except it is a lot simpler."

Assessments of the Business Environment

In the opinion of AMC's management, big changes in the business environment do not affect AMC as directly as its larger competitors. With only a 2 to 3 percent share of the domestic market, AMC is not greatly concerned about major socioeconomic issues that might influence car sales.

The impact of government regulations on AMC does not appear to be as profound and immediate as the impact on GM. This is because AMC is heavily dependent on vendors for its emissions, safety, and fuel economy technology. In addition, because AMC's passenger car line already consists mostly of compact and subcompact models, the company does not need to undertake the sort of massive down-sizing programs underway at the Big Three. Consequently, AMC's assessments of the business environment are limited in scope and involve only small parts of its management staff. As already noted, the company frequently makes use of outside research firms to supply data. For example, for its economic forecasting AMC relies on data supplied by one or two economic research firms. It also purchases demographic studies from the outside. These data are ordered and used by members of the marketing and financial staffs. But, unlike the Big Three who back up most of this research with similar research done internally, AMC's staff usually limits itself to evaluating and integrating the data supplied.

The marketing and product planning staffs of AMC, in particular, relied on outside research during the planning stage of the Pacer in order to obtain data about such trends as the consumer move from standard-sized cars into smaller cars and consumer dissatisfaction with subcompacts; AMC also commissioned a series of consumer clinics to determine consumer preferences. As a result of this outside research, AMC's product planning and marketing staffs developed specifications for an "urban car" that combined small exterior dimensions with a roomy interior.

American Motors Corporation employs a small government affairs staff that is responsible for monitoring government regulations. The findings of this staff are directly fed to the technical staffs of the product engineering, vehicle emissions, and safety groups. However, these staffs have only a small-scale involvement in safety, emissions, and fuel economy research and undertake little or no advanced research themselves. Many "mandatory" components are purchased in ready form from General Motors, such as the energy-absorbent steering column, the catalytic converter, and the air pump. Whatever research is done is usually done in cooperation with a supplier—AMC provides the concept and specifications and the supplier develops the hardware. American Motors Corporation's energy-absorbent bumper systems were a result of this type of cooperation.

Typically, AMC does not undertake any "anticipatory" research but rather awaits the regulatory outcome before contacting suppliers for a joint development. This practice of not committing extensive resources to the monitoring and anticipating of regulations is currently being used in the matter of side-impact protection.

Clearly, AMC is not in a position to support an extensive staff to monitor changes in the environment. Instead, its efforts in this regard are incidental and on a small scale. Nor does it have some kind of organizational entity along the lines of the external-factors group recently created at Ford Motor Company to monitor and assess changes in the environment. Instead, AMC's assessments of the business environment take place in various parts of the organization and are dictated by particular needs rather than being a general, ongoing activity.

Likewise, AMC has not established a formal process for the continuous evaluation of its internal strengths and weaknesses. Outside the company's policy committee little or no effort is undertaken in this direction. (For instance, at no stage during the planning and development of the Pacer did AMC attempt to determine whether it had the necessary strength to promote such a novel styling and vehicle concept as that embodied in the Pacer.)

Product Planning

Because of AMC's small product line the company's product planning process is fairly simple. It revolves around a five-year planning cycle and places a heavy emphasis on the updating of current models. Rarely does AMC develop a completely new model. The most recent one is the Pacer, introduced in 1975. The Pacer illustrates how closely involved all levels of management are when a new product is being planned.

Planning for the Pacer started in 1970 within the product committee which, at that time, included the chairman, president, and the vice presidents of finance, corporate staffs, marketing, and product. This committee decided that a new model had to be added to the AMC product line and established as a guideline that it should be something totally new and unique with a maximum profit potential.

With this guideline as a starting point, a joint team of product planning and marketing staff members began to work on the specifications. The first question to be resolved was in what area the new product had to be positioned for maximum profit. Two areas were identified: the low-volume, luxury line and the high-volume, small-car line. Because a luxury car did not fit into AMC's corporate strategy and the company did not have the necessary financial and engineering resources available, the second option was selected.

The joint product planning/marketing team contracted with an outside firm to do consumer research on such trends as the move down from standard-sized cars to smaller cars and buyer dissatisfaction with small cars. The results of this research indicated that there was an opportunity for a small car that offered comfort and roominess. Subsequently, members of the planning team formulated the "urban car" concept—a small car that offered the interior dimensions of a standard-sized car. It was felt that this would appeal to a market where fuel economy was of lesser importance than comfort. Proposed government regulations on peripheral vision and side protection were taken into account in the specification by the inclusion in the design of large window areas and side-door beams. Manufacturing engineers were then asked to submit a tooling proposal. Together with finance staff members they prepared an estimate of the development costs. A position paper was then developed, including the basic specifications of the projected car, a price positioning, and a market positioning, as well as several alternatives, each with its pros and cons.

Approximately one year after the start of the process the whole package was submitted to the product committee for approval. Here the decision to go ahead with the urban-car concept was made, although at the expense of such alternatives as adding a proposed van to the Jeep line.

In the ensuing year the planning team, in cooperation with members of the engineering, manufacturing, purchasing, styling, and finance staffs, further refined the specifications for the urban-car concept. It should be noted that a final decision was made on which concept to pursue in a very early stage of the planning process. In this respect AMC's product planning process distinguishes itself from that used in other companies where a product decision is often made after several alternative prototypes have been developed. The styling and engineering staffs were then given a set of "hard points" around which to design the car. Such engineering alternatives as front wheel drive, independent rear suspension, and the Wankel engine were rejected by either the engineering or the finance staff because of the cost involved or because no domestic suppliers were available to provide them. A four-door model was rejected by styling and engineering because it would become too heavy and because the basic styling did not lend itself to this configuration.

Meanwhile, the marketing staff continued to organize consumer clinics to further determine the positioning and appeal of the new model. Approximately one year before the new-model introduction the specifications were "frozen" and the car entered the final development stage. As the work progressed, monthly meetings were held with the product committee to review the progress made. When compared to the Big Three, the number of people who participated in the process is very small. The largest groups involved were styling and engineering with approximately eighty people in all. Seldom were the finance, product planning, and marketing staffs represented by more than three people each. Because of the small group of people involved there was a high degree of informality in the process, and unscheduled meetings were frequently held between various staff members to work out a specific problem. Further, it was not unusual for the chairman or the president to drop into the styling studio and discuss the latest progress. The name of the new car was decided through an informal balloting system in which each member of the product committee was asked to submit two names to the director of marketing services.

The process through which a model update is planned at AMC does not differ much from the process of planning for a new car. Because there were not enough resources available to develop another new car in 1974, the product committee decided instead to update a current model, the Hornet. The planning team submitted a proposal to upgrade this model after studying the success of the Ford Granada/Mercury Monarch and comparable GM models. After this proposal was approved by the product committee, the task was primarily carried out by styling, and the Concord evolved.

Pricing

Pricing is another area where AMC's decision-making process is uncomplicated and informal and involves a small number of people. Pricing decisions are made within two overall parameters: prices set by the price leader of a particular market segment where AMC intends to position its product and AMC profit objectives.

In every segment of the U.S. passenger car market where AMC has products, it competes with much larger competitors, one of which is usually the price leader. Therefore, in AMC's decision-making process no consideration is given to what effect AMC's price setting may have on the size of the market or to any macroeconomic impacts. This eliminates the need for an extensive effort by an economic staff to participate in price setting. In most cases the market situation gives AMC a ceiling above which its own prices cannot be set.

Recognizing AMC's weak market position and lack of resources to carry out an aggressive new-model policy, the company's strategy is to maximize profits at whatever volume it can achieve. In several instances in the past AMC has attempted to increase its volume by implementing a price cut in one of its product lines, but rarely has the company managed to maintain the resulting volume increase for a long time. Rather than trying once more to increase volume at any cost, the policy committee has decided, instead, to upgrade AMC's model line and to improve unit profit margins. The Concord, introduced in 1978, is the first example of this new strategy.

The pricing of the Concord was an inherent part of the product planning program. Through the consumer clinics the marketing staff estimated the perceived worth of the new model and prepared an estimate of the expenses that would be incurred to market it. Meanwhile, product development engineers prepared projections of the production costs. Because the Concord involved the upgrading of a current model, these projections took the form of projected cost increments over the current model. Early on, AMC's suppliers were invited to submit cost estimates for this development effort.

Throughout the process the marketing people and product engineers met in the controller's office and, through an informal give-and-take process, made decisions as to whether the price should be lowered to increase volume potential and whether they should try to lower the price of supplied components and trim costs to improve profit margins. The result of the interaction among finance, marketing, and product engineering was a white paper with several base-price alternatives, each with a range of options and their profit potentials. This paper formed part of a package that was presented to the product committee. Approximately twelve months before the introduction of the Concord the product committee decided to keep its base price low but to add an extensive list of optional equipment that could bring the price to more than $5,000.

As with the decision-making process in general, price setting at AMC is characterized by a high degree of informality. The frequent and informal interaction among finance, product engineering, and marketing people is facilitated by the small size of the staffs. Because the company does not believe that it is necessary to engage in extensive economic analysis and projections, the process is also fairly simple and straightforward.

Impact of External Pressures
on Decision Making

In recent years several trends in AMC's environment have had a noticeable impact on the company's decision making. The most important of these have been high rates of inflation and government regulations on safety, emissions, and fuel economy.

High increases in the costs of materials, labor, and components have had an especially severe impact on AMC because of its small size (relative to its competitors), its heavy reliance on outside suppliers, and its weaker financial situation. Being the smallest U.S. car manufacturer, AMC's ability to recoup cost increases through increased prices is limited by the prices set by its competitors, notably GM, which, as the growth in personal disposable income slows down, is willing to internally absorb a substantive portion of these increases rather than passing them all on to the consumer. Because GM has a much larger product line and broader product mix than does AMC, it is able to do this through increased volume efficiency and shifts in its product mix toward more profitable items.

The problem at AMC is compounded by its weak bargaining position relative to its suppliers. Because it is heavily dependent on these suppliers for many vital components, the suppliers are in a position to pass most of their cost increases on to AMC. Faced with this cost-price squeeze, AMC looks for an internal means of reducing costs as well as the pressures on its profit margins. Reducing costs has become a primary consideration in AMC's decision making, with efforts being made to further reduce the size of its finance and marketing staffs as well as its product engineering and development staffs, even though government regulations translate into substantial new engineering requirements. In the product development process, constant attention is paid to the possibility of reducing costs through material substitution. In the manufacturing area AMC recently decided to concentrate all its car assembly operations in its Kenosha, Wisconsin, assembly plant.

Traditionally, AMC's product policy has been to look for the market niches neglected by the Big Three. In this way AMC built up a product base primarily in the small-car end of the market. But as the Big Three are being forced today to move into that same segment, AMC has no option but to meet its larger competitors head-on. Thus, AMC has decided to position its new Concord in direct competition with comparable products from Ford, GM, and Chrysler.

Previously, in the case of the Pacer, AMC attempted to position this new model as a unique product that did not compete directly with any product offered by the Big Three.

Government regulations have changed AMC's process of bargaining with its suppliers. Despite the company's heavy dependence on suppliers, it has often been able to bargain with them and have them absorb at least part of their own increases in costs. Although AMC has relatively stable relationships with its suppliers, it can always use the threat of going to an alternative supplier or using another material or component as a bargaining point. However, with equipment that is mandated by the law, AMC has no such alternative and suppliers of this equipment are usually able to dictate their own prices.

Government regulations have also impacted AMC's capital investment decision making. The portion of AMC's capital budget that is devoted to compliance with government standards continues to grow and reduces the funds available for model updates or new models. In the past AMC would devote a portion of its yearly budget alternately to the update of its Jeep line and to its passenger car line. Essentially, the Jeep product line has remained the same since its acquisition in 1968, and AMC's expenditures on the line have been limited to slight model updates and some proliferation. However, new federal fuel economy standards for utility vehicles will force AMC to make substantial investments on the Jeep line in order to have it comply with these new standards—it will cost AMC an estimated $120 million to modify and down-size the various Jeep models. In recent years Jeep has become AMC's major profit contributor. Accordingly, AMC has decided to give first priority to transformation of the line. Expenditures on its passenger car line will be limited to slight model updates, and no new models will be introduced for at least three more years.

15 Chrysler Corporation

Overview

Chrysler's net sales in 1977 exceeded $16 billion, which makes the company a very large one by any standards. However, within the automotive industry Chrysler is considered to be the underdog, by itself and its competitors alike.

This feeling of smallness despite size pervades throughout the Chrysler organization and influences the company's organizational structure and the character of its decision making. At Chrysler there are no elaborate structures built around separate car divisions or sophisticated mechanisms for scanning the business and social environment. As one official stated, "We cannot afford the luxury of following exactly what is going on in our environment; we let Ford and GM do that for us." In its cost-cutting moves in 1974 and 1975, Chrysler disbanded its entire economics department so that today the company operates without any economic analysis or environmental assessment team.

Essentially, Chrysler's organizational structure is highly centralized with the car divisions being only separate entities at the retail level. Consequently, strategic decision making is concentrated in a small number of people. Strategic and operating decisions are made by the nine members of the Chrysler operations committee, by the chairman and president as a team, or by the chairman alone. The whole process of decision making is characterized by a high degree of informality that is facilitated by the straightforward nature of the organization and the small number of people involved.

Strategic Emphasis

Chrysler was founded by a self-educated engineer and great innovator, Walter Chrysler, who created the company that bears his name by rescuing the Maxwell Motor Company from financial collapse in the early 1920s. During the next thirty years engineering excellence became Chrysler's prime objective as the company remained under the leadership of engineers and mechanics. In the 1950s Chrysler changed its focus for the first time when under Lester Colbert, its president and chief executive officer whose background was in marketing and sales, its objective became that of being the styling leader in the industry. In the process Chrysler lost its reputation for outstanding engineering.

In the 1960s, under the leadership of Lynn Townsend, chairman and chief executive officer, Chrysler shifted its emphasis to expansion in order to become

129

a worldwide producer of automobiles. Townsend's objective was to put Chrysler on an equal overall footing with Ford and GM. To accomplish this, he established car operations in Europe, South Africa, Australia, and South America; at home he expanded Chrysler's product line to cover each segment in which Ford and GM were represented. This expansion was done at the expense of financial stability and manufacturing efficiency, and it neglected the updating and improvement of manufacturing facilities. Consequently, the manufacturing cost differential from which Chrysler suffered, relative to Ford and GM, only widened. Further, because of a highly leveraged financial structure, Chrysler's earnings pattern became erratic and very sensitive to economic downturns.

During the recession of 1974-1975 Chrysler experienced a financial crisis, and a new management team took over. Under the leadership of John Riccardo, chairman, and Eugene A. Cafiero, president, a period of consolidation took place. Money-losing operations were sold or consolidated, and rigorous cost-cutting measures were taken, reducing the size of staffs and all but eliminating the separate car divisions. Today, under the direction of Cafiero, who has an extensive background in manufacturing, Chrysler is updating its complete production apparatus in an attempt to close the gap in manufacturing efficiency between itself and its two larger competitors.

The Process of Decision Making

Traditionally, Chrysler has been led by strong-willed, authoritarian individuals, and decisions have been made by one person alone, or possibly with a few advisors, with little or no delegation of responsibility made outside this small group. Lynn Townsend was no exception to this rule. He exerted control over practically every aspect of operations. The organizational structure of the company remained very centralized and vertical in nature, with little depth at the middle management level and all power concentrated at the top.

In the last years of Townsend's reign (which lasted until 1975) the system started to change. Under Riccardo, who became president in 1970, some middle management functions, notably product planning and development, were strengthened and expanded. Then, in 1975, just before his early retirement, Townsend announced the formation of an operations committee including the chairman, the president, the newly appointed executive vice president (Cafiero), and four vice presidents.

After Townsend's departure Chrysler was for the first time headed by a management team—Riccardo and Cafiero—rather than by one man. This team further increased the division and delegation of responsibilities throughout the company. A simple organizational structure was developed with all the staff functions reporting to the chairman and all the operations to the president. The new team announced that the operations committee would become the forum for most operating decisions. Today this nine-member committee includes the chairman; president; executive vice president of North American automotive; executive vice president of engineering, product development, and purchasing; group vice president of nonautomotive; group vice president of international; vice president and comptroller; vice president and treasurer; and vice president of public affairs. This diffusion of decision-making authority has allowed the chairman and the president to devote more time to corporate strategic and planning issues.

Apart from the operations committee a series of new committees was also created, combining members of the operations committee with lower-level managers to report to the chairman and president on a variety of issues. One such committee is the vehicle safety and reliability committee, which includes people from the manufacturing, engineering, purchasing, legal, and comptroller functions. This committee convenes monthly to discuss safety and reliability issues and may, for example, make a de facto decision regarding a product recall. Only when its opinion conflicts with a stand taken by a government agency do the chairman and president make the final decision.

Chrysler's decision-making process has changed over the years. For example, in 1973 when Lynn Townsend decided that Chrysler was not going to produce a minicar because the market for these vehicles was not profitable enough, his two close assistants, Riccardo and Cafiero, were in accordance with him. But when the market for subcompacts rapidly increased after the fuel crisis, Cafiero changed his mind and wanted to start development of a Chrysler subcompact. Townsend refused to approve the project until shortly before his retirement. Today no product decisions are made by one single individual; instead, they are carefully evaluated by the nine-member operations committee. Every proposal concerning a new model, its packaging, manufacturing cost, and pricing is submitted to the operations committee where final decisions on these issues are made.

Planning

Chrysler's growth in the 1960s was achieved without an underlying long-range plan. Foreign subsidiaries were established without any regard to whether they could achieve synergistic effects. At home Chrysler's product strategy closely followed the strategies of Ford and GM, matching each of their new models with an additional new Chrysler model. In 1970 when the decision was made to increasingly emphasize compact cars, it was done without considering the long-range effects this policy would have on Chrysler's product mix and profitability. As already noted, at Chrysler engineers had traditionally dominated the product planning and marketing functions, a situation that continued under Lynn Townsend, and manufacturing efficiency was allowed to deteriorate.

In 1973 a first step was made to reduce the influence of engineering on product planning and increase the importance of the planning function. Under the direction of President Riccardo, the corporate product planning and development functions were strengthened by consolidating them with advanced engineering and research into a single department headed by a person who, significantly, had no engineering background. The new department head had top-level responsibility and reported directly to the president. At the same time Chrysler expanded and strengthened its consumer research function.

When Riccardo and Cafiero took control in 1975, one task they set out to accomplish was the development of Chrysler's first all-encompassing planning system. To do this, they asked all people from management levels upward to develop a plan and set their own objectives. For the first time a set of corporate objectives was formulated as well as a program to reduce the number of different parts and Chrysler's manufacturing cost penalty.

In 1977 Chrysler's first long-range plan was on paper. It specified that Chrysler would remain a producer of a complete line of cars in order to offset smaller profit margins on its subcompacts with higher profit margins on its full-sized models. It also called for achieving improvements in Chrysler's CAFE through a series of down-sizings. As for Chrysler's manufacturing efficiency, this would be improved through extensive modernization of all production facilities. Finally, Chrysler's new models would be geared toward upgrading the company's buyer profile which had traditionally been dominated by low-income, older, blue-collar consumers.

Impact of External Pressures
on Decision Making

The primary impact of external pressures on Chrysler's decision making is a reduction in the number of options open to the company, and consequently a limited flexibility in the kinds of decisions it can make. For example, in 1974 when Lynn Townsend came to realize how much the strategy of competing across the board with Ford and GM had cost the company, he announced that from then on Chrysler would be more selective in its product areas, focusing only on those products where it performed best. However, when the fuel economy standards for 1981-1985 were announced, the company had no choice but to compete head-on with its two larger competitors since it was felt that if Chrysler was to meet the CAFE standards and not be reduced to the size of an AMC, it had to produce a full range of automobiles covering the same segments as Ford and GM.

Chrysler's decision to drop the Imperial line in 1975 was fairly straight-forward after it determined that the low sales volume of the model did not warrant additional marketing and merchandising costs. Today the decision to drop a model line would be more complicated since subcompacts are needed to meet the CAFE standards, compacts are an area where Chrysler is strongest, and the new full-sized cars are needed to offset the low profit margins on the smaller models.

Reduced flexibility is also felt in Chrysler's investment decision making. Chrysler uses the notion of payback period in deciding on investment proposals. It used to be that for a proposal to be accepted, it needed to show a payback period of fourteen months or less. Today a nonregulatory-related proposal needs to show a payback period of eight months at the most to have any chance of being considered for adoption.

16 Ford Motor Company

A Formal/Informal Style
of Decision Making

Ford Motor Company, founded in 1903 by Henry Ford, stands alongside a few other large U.S. corporations, namely, W.R. Grace & Co. and McDonnell Douglas, where the top management position has traditionally been held by descendants of the original founder. It is also a company where the decision-making process commingles informal and formal procedures. Henry Ford II, the grandson of Henry Ford, as chairman of the board and chief executive officer, is a visible corporate figure who has established himself as Ford's leader, chief negotiator, and spokesman and whose management style over the years can best be described as one of direct intervention. For example, in 1973 when Ford Motor Company decided to take advantage of the changing political environment in Spain, that country's lower labor costs, and its interest in new capital investment and invested $734 million (to establish manufacturing and assembly operations inside the country and a supply operation outside) in order to penetrate the southern European market with an entirely new product, the Fiesta, this represented not only the single largest investment made by the company up to that time but a high-risk strategy as well. The success of this venture was largely due to the direct involvement and participation of Henry Ford II in negotiations with the Spanish government as well as with King Juan Carlos I. Ford used this same approach of direct intervention by traveling to South Africa in 1977 to assess for himself the magnitude of the problems in that country as well as their significance for company operations in both South Africa and the United States.

The direct management style of Henry Ford II also carries over to corporate decision making in that many major corporate decisions are the product of his own thinking and independent assessment of the options available—and are often the result of his own personal, hands-on experience and access to information on a particular issue or situation. Still, in making most major decisions, Henry Ford II is briefed by a staff of advisors and sometimes acts on recommendations proposed by one or more advisory committees. Nonetheless, it is important to note that he is not likely to make a major decision concerning the direction of the company unless he personally feels comfortable with that decision.

Henry Ford II also fills a direct liaison role between Ford Motor Company and the U.S. government and, in this capacity, has sometimes been influential in determining industry direction. For example, in 1972 when the National

Highway Traffic Safety Administration proposed the use of passive restraints for 1974-model year cars, Henry Ford II was instrumental in influencing the government to approve a Ford-designed alternative—a front seat belt starter switch (interlock) system.

Despite Henry Ford II's informal, personal management and decision-making style, Ford Motor Company has some formalized planning procedures, such as product planning, that date back to 1953. Because product planning is a basic ingredient in the strategic decision making for any automaker, Ford's product planning process and decision making are discussed in detail further. However, it is relevant to indicate here that decisions involving new-product introductions have more often been the result of a procedural planning process where final product approval is given by the head of the product division involved and a member of senior corporate management simply signs off on it. While most operating decisions are decentralized and the responsibility of division heads, final product decisions may be initiated by a division's management, but final product approval is required by senior management. An example of this situation is the North American Automotive Operations (NAAO) group's recommendation to add the Futura/Zephyr Z-7 to its new, basic Fairmont/Zephyr line in order to enrich it with a "sportier" configuration. Because the expenditure involved exceeded the level at which NAAO could decide on its own, final approval had to be given by the finance committee.

The Structure and Process of Management Decision Making

A number of structural and organizational changes have been made at the senior level of Ford Motor Company since the spring of 1977. Many of these were initiated by Henry Ford II who feels the need to provide a smooth management transition when he steps down as Ford's chief executive officer in 1980 and as its chairman in 1983 (when he is sixty-five years old), as well as a more organized system for corporate decision making to cope with the growing complexity of the external environment in which the company operates and the concomitant risks and uncertainties.

The OCE, the CS&A, and the Advisory Committees

In April 1977 the office of chief executive (OCE) was organized to broaden Ford Motor Company's decision-making base. Members of the OCE (until June 1978) included Henry Ford II, chairman and chief executive officer, responsible for relations with external forces (that is, stockholders, governments, and directors) and retaining veto power when a consensus could not be reached; Philip Caldwell, chairman of the board, responsible for strategic and business planning integration and overall policy development and implementation; and Lee A. Iacocca, chief operating officer, responsible for operations and the operating committee. In July 1977 the office of corporate strategy and analysis (CS&A) was established (and, within it, three groups—business planning, product planning, and external factors) to serve the OCE and support its efforts to manage strategic decisions more effectively. Then, in a surprise move in June 1978, Henry Ford II reorganized the OCE to include his brother, William C. Ford, as chairman of the executive committee as well as vice president of product design. This move was viewed as a means of ensuring a family successor. In addition, Caldwell was named deputy chief executive officer with Iacocca reporting to him. Then, in July 1978 Henry Ford II again surprised everyone by firing Iacocca as president of Ford Motor Company, claiming there was no room in the company for both Iacocca and himself. These moves clearly indicate the control and influence that Henry Ford II exercises over the company. Finally, in September 1978 Caldwell was named president of Ford Motor Company in addition to his other responsibilities.

As already noted, Ford's advisory committees play an important role in the strategic decision-making process by providing Henry Ford II and/or the OCE with considerations and/or recommendations from both line and staff on matters requiring top-level consent. To further improve the effectiveness of and support provided by the advisory committees, in February 1978 several changes were made to their structure, responsibilities, and membership. One of the changes most relevant to this discussion was redesignation of the policy committee, the principal advisory committee to the OCE on policy and strategy matters, as the policy and strategy committee and the establishment of seven subcommittees: design, engineering and research, product planning, marketing, manufacturing and supply, human resources, and public and governmental affairs. In addition, the functions of the CS&A were extended to allow it to act as the liaison between the policy and strategy committee and the OCE. Together, these changes represent a quantum jump for Ford Motor Company's strategic planning system. The objectives to be achieved through this restructuring process are to allow the OCE, supported by the CS&A, to respond proactively to increasing regulatory, competitive, and other external pressures and to effectively manage the company's tremendous capital expenditures program and maintain a stable dividend growth.

Strategy Issues Studies and
Planning Mechanisms

Several of the strategy development procedures/activities through which Ford Motor Company does its strategic decision-making are described.

Agenda of Strategic Issues. Through a "circular" iterative process the CS&A and the OCE jointly develop an agenda of strategic issues (about thirty issues covering such matters as energy, platinum-group metals supply, and Japanese-U.S. trade). To compile this agenda, the CS&A initially solicits (by letter) topics of interest from various sources and levels within the company and asks for suggestions on how to deal with these effectively. The CS&A, rather than studying these issues itself, assigns lead responsibility to the most appropriate in-house group for examining a particular issue and its impact and developing a strategy or action plan to follow in resolving it. It then submits the results produced by each group to the policy and strategy committee for review before seeking final approval from the OCE. Some strategies may necessitate immediate, short-term action while others may require a ten-year plan for long-term study and resolution. Because members of the OCE are also members (formal or ex officio) of the policy and strategy committee, final approval is generally not a problem. As individual issues are studied, determined, and action plans implemented, they are struck from the agenda and replaced by other strategic issues.

Task Studies. The external-factors group of the CS&A is responsible for task studies which, like the agenda issues studies, are conducted by various of the thirteen corporate staff groups (such as public affairs, advanced engineering, scientific research, and supply). The CS&A's external-factors group develops assumptions on those strategic issues solicited from various organizational levels which it considers to be germane to successful company operations. These guidelines serve as a point of departure for the group assigned to a particular issue. The external factors group continues to provide assistance to the various staff groups in analyzing and developing task papers. Task studies generally take two to two-and-one-half months to complete and are scheduled for presentation to the policy and strategy committee in July of each year.

After the external-factors group presents a general overview of all the task studies to the policy and strategy committee, followed by an in-depth presentation of particularly significant issues, an impact analysis of those issues considered to be especially pertinent to Ford's operations is conducted jointly by the representatives from each of the thirteen corporate staff groups and the policy and strategy committee to determine and project both the quantitative and qualitative impact of these issues on the industry and/or the company. Several techniques and sources are used to develop a consensus on any particular issue (for example, Delphi technique, open discussion, outside studies). These critical task studies are then analyzed further by corporate staff personnel and presented to the policy and strategy committee before final approval from the OCE is sought. Because this entire process is relatively new, further refinements are likely to be made as Ford's management continues to use it.

Ten-Year Business Plans. The CS&A is also responsible for administering the ten-year business plans prepared by each Ford Motor Company division. These plans include broad strategies to be carried out during a specified ten-year period and are based on information developed and submitted by the individual divisions to the CS&A's external-factors group and business planning group (market share, ROI, and business opportunities data). (The business planning group actually oversees and administers the entire business planning process.) These plans are conceptual and directional in nature rather than quantitative, and they are relatively brief. They essentially represent broad product, marketing, and manufacturing approaches for each division. [Our research into the corporate strategies employed by other U.S. companies shows that the more progressive strategy-oriented companies (for example, International Paper and Union Carbide) use long-range strategic business planning approaches similar to that used by Ford.]

Five-Year Profit Projections and Financial Strategies. Each division is also asked to prepare a five-year profit projection and financial strategy which are then reviewed by the finance committee. To assist the divisions in preparing these, the economics department analyzes computerized data and develops corporate assumptions related to consumer demand, sales volume, national economic growth, and so forth, to be incorporated into the plans and tied into the corporate budgetary and resource allocation process.

Assessment of External Factors. Although individual groups or committees were organized to provide input to the planning process concerning external issues, prior to the establishment of the CS&A and the organization of its external factors, business planning, and product planning groups, no one group in Ford Motor Company could put together a cohesive picture of the company's near-term and long-term future and assess the impact of external influences on corporate policies and strategies. In addition, prior to the restructuring in 1977, the assessment of external factors was probably the least well organized of the planning functions at Ford. Essentially, the main function of the external-factors group is to translate for senior management the significance of external factors to the company and establish a track into the future. This is more than a paper exercise, however, in that it provides a critical element of the decision-making process.

The CS&A's external-factors group includes twelve senior professionals. (A European external-factors group similarly monitors external factors in that environment.) It develops a best or most likely case as well as a possible alternative for the external environment assumptions (altogether approximately twenty-five pages in length) to be included in the division's ten-year business plan. In developing these cases, the external-factors group sometimes uses outside specialists as data resources; for example, Chase Econometrics is under contract to the economics department for volume modeling and market segmentation activities. Such data would be used by the CS&A.

The external-factors group is concerned with two different kinds of outside factors that impact Ford's operations: technical/regulatory influences and commercial influences. The technical/regulatory influences include such agencies and issues as:

OSHA, EPA, NHTSA (relative to the direction in which they are actually moving, not where they claim to be going, in order to "unbutton" underlying assumptions and obtain a better understanding of the nature of the regulatory environment)

Technical communications (for example, new opportunities for transmitting information within Ford)

The availability of critical materials (such as platinum-group metals)

Gas rationing and global energy supplies (for example, supply-demand data analyses to determine cost per barrel)

The commercial influences include such matters as political movements, demographic changes (for example, age/family status/population dispersions), the U.S. rate of growth, dealer service and franchise matters, and insurance and credit issues.

Assessment of Internal Strengths and Weaknesses. Ford Motor Company has a formal process of self-criticism at the corporate level for identifying the company's strengths and weaknesses—another element critical to strategic planning and decision making. In addition, an informal assessment is incorporated into the impact analysis segment of the task studies described. This assessment is also used in the development of overall issue papers. An assessment of this type is essential for optimal resource allocation and for evaluating diversification strategies and opportunities.

Product Planning. Ford has experienced increasing difficulties in developing a profitable product mix because of growing pressures from the regulatory environment as well as the complexities of its current R&D activities. Moreover, prior to the restructuring of the OCE and the advisory committees, Ford's executive management did not participate regularly in developing long-term product strategy alternatives. Instead, approval was made on one or two alternatives of a predigested product development program which left the lower organizational levels satisfied, but top management less so. Consequently, in July

1977 Ford Motor Company raised product design to the senior management level of decision making and added six months' lead time to the implementation phase (involving business strategy development and advanced product planning, performed by the product planning group of CS&A, as discussed below) of its product development program, thereby extending the product planning cycle from eighty-five months to ninety-one months. Because of this change Ford, in 1978, should be in the initial planning phase for its model year 1985 cars. However, because of regulatory changes and uncertainties as well as internal difficulties, it is still planning for the 1983-1984 model years. Product planning decisions are being put off for as long as possible in order to prevent the company from becoming locked into an untenable position while operating in an uncertain environment.

The product planning group is an advisory group responsible for defining product needs and for providing the OCE with product information based on an assessment of future internal and external factors (as provided by the external-factors group). To accomplish this, the product planning group develops a series of strategies, outlining the strengths and weaknesses of each of them, that shows current product line thinking, outlines three or four basic alternatives, and presents several variations of each alternative. Once the broad product direction is determined, the advanced vehicle development group (AVD—now directly under product design, the responsibility of William C. Ford) designs the hardware for the Ford cars of the future.

Advanced vehicle development is responsible for recommending car size, product configuration, image, cost and investment objectives, feasibility, and the tradeoffs involved. It develops either a mechanical prototype (a modification of an existing car) or a handmade replica (a style-prototype driveable car). Engineering then designs the hardware and its engineering processes.

It is important to note here that the ultimate responsibility for product development rests with division operations. Each major group at Ford (for example, NAAO car and truck, European car and truck, tractors, electronics, and some manufacturing units) does its own product planning. Anywhere along the way during the implementation phase and up to execution of the production program in the twenty-eighth month prior to product introduction, NAAO car manufacturing, for example, can reject a product concept developed in the product planning process. If this happens, justification for the rejection must be referred to the OCE for approval. It should be noted here that NAAO would be directly involved from the earliest stages of the product planning process since it is the group that knows the most about existing Ford products.

In approximately five years (the sixty-fourth month) prior to a given model-year introduction, after a review of the ten-year product strategy alternatives and the five-year profit projections, a product development strategy is determined by product planning and the divisions. As in the business strategy development, this process is an iterative one. The objective is to simply have a five-year product plan that can be reviewed each year and added to, although in practice this is very difficult given the changing regulatory environment. A final financing strategy and specific product concept are also developed at this time. A division then has five months to change or correct the design concept before the production program is executed.

Investment Analysis and Capital Allocation. Return on investment (after taxes) is the key financial determinant of capital resource allocation at Ford Motor Company today. Prior to 1974 the company was able to employ funds for discretionary programs and accept a low-return project to protect its market share or increase market penetration, as done with the Fiesta program in Europe. However, because of the large amount of capital needed to respond to U.S. regulatory requirements and the low returns the company experiences with regulatory programs, Ford has been forced to increase its ROI hurdle rate for discretionary programs (high-margin, "luxury" product options which traditionally have been a profitable source of revenue for all the automakers) 10 to 15 percentage points above that of other major U.S. corporations reviewed in this book.

Because Ford Motor Company can no longer fund pure styling, it instead closely plots sales to determine when a low-cost face-lifting is needed on a particular product line. Policy guidelines relative to ROI hurdle rates and resource allocation are developed by the finance committee, with assistance from the economics department, and advisory business strategy input is provided by the CS&A.

**Impact of External Pressures on
Decision Making**

A rich product mix and large sales volumes are key to General Motors' profitability. Ford Motor Company has struggled for over three decades to combat GM's relative advantage in the domestic passenger car market and to counter it somewhat by aggressively pursuing the truck and overseas markets. Until 1975 Ford's product decisions were primarily directed to bolster its competitive and financial advantage relative to GM and to position itself to be able to react quickly to GM's marketing initiatives. After enactment of the Energy Policy and Conservation Act of 1975, this strategy shifted as the regulatory environment made it more difficult for Ford to make long-term product decisions and increased the company's reluctance to reduce its operating flexibility by making product decisions before it had to or was ready to.

According to John Deaver, manager of Ford's economics department, product-mix decisions are now determined by the number of large and medium-sized cars the company believes it can sell, and then by the number of

small cars it needs to produce/sell in order to meet CAFE requiremen
According to Deaver, small cars are not profitable; therefore, Ford has not real
been interested in having small-car sales comprise its major market share.
Nevertheless, Ford must make a major production and marketing effort in the
small-car segment of the market in order to maintain its ability to sell large and
medium-sized cars.

Ford is primarily interested in selling (1) a minimum number of small cars
to meet CAFE requirements; (2) a minimum number of high-cost components
(such as air bags and catalytic converters) needed for regulatory compliance but
which reduce the overall profit margin on a vehicle; and (3) a maximum number
of larger cars and higher-margin optional "luxury" items. Consequently, Ford
has relegated to the corporate decision-making level many of what were formerly
decentralized, somewhat routine product planning decisions. In order for Ford
to continue to be profitable enough to meet shareholders' expectations and the
company's own future equity needs, the company had to assume a proactive
posture at the senior management level for dealing with the external environment. Centralized issue management and decentralized product line responsibility, coupled with a continued relative flexibility, is Ford's response to a
regulatory environment.

17 General Motors Corporation

Overview

General Motors stresses the informality and collaborative nature of its decision-making process. The company has no formal strategic planning function as does Ford Motor Company. Further, most of its important decisions are made through a complex web of corporate committees that in most companies would probably result in a bureaucratic morass. Decision making in many companies—and GM does not claim to be an exception—tends to be done by a few key people in unlikely places such as restaurants, airplanes, and office corridors. However, many observers believe that GM is able to make the democratic process work more effectively than other companies because of some basic values deeply embedded in the GM organization.

In unraveling GM's decision-making process, the focus will be on product decisions in order to trace whatever systematic steps exist. In doing this, three factors affecting GM decisions are described: the climate and basic principles of the organization affecting the people who make decisions, the framework and process by which product decisions are made, and the key influencers of GM product decisions.

Climate and Organization for Decision Making

Between 1910 and 1920 the fledgling corporation of General Motors struggled for survival against the industry leader, Ford Motor Company. At that time GM held less than 10 percent of the market while Ford consistently held better than 50 percent, largely attributable to the success of the Model T, a low-priced "people's car." In 1920 GM's market share dropped to about 5 percent while Ford's continued at 55 percent, even though GM, with six divisions, was competing against only three Ford divisions. Alfred P. Sloan, GM's chairman, perceived that part of the company's problem was too much overlap, waste, and redundancy among its five relatively independent car divisions and the lack of coordinated corporate product and financial policies. Sloan and his colleagues envisioned a market for automobiles that was about to undergo significant growth because of (1) an increase in the number of paved roads, (2) the growth of the used-car market, (3) the introduction of bank financing, and (4) the development of a "closed body" design. Sloan decided that if GM was going to compete effectively with Ford in this "new" market for autos, a major restructuring of GM's approach to policy making had to be accomplished. It was then that Sloan, the architect of GM's basic management structure and philosophy, decided that the company had to exercise strong central controls over decisions having a financial impact on the corporation and, particularly, had to develop a more coordinated, rational overall corporate product policy.

In restructuring GM, Sloan introduced new principles that became the basis for GM's management system for years to come. Many people believe that these principles, which are still very much alive today, are the primary reason for GM's remarkable success over the years. Some of the more salient ones are discussed.

Centralized Policy Making

All major policy decisions at GM are made at central headquarters. These include major product decisions such as new-model designs, promotional programs, new-product development plans, new technology or new components, the selection of lead divisions, the allocation of R&D and capital funds for new-product development, and the selection of plants to manufacture/assemble new models. As a way of enforcing and controlling adherence to corporate policy, GM also established strong central control over all capital allocations. The original purpose of this control was to ensure that GM's five major car divisions pursued an integrated business strategy and that redundancy was kept to a minimum. Today, because of the enormous problems in meeting federal standards, the trend toward centralized decision making and policy control is greater than ever before.

Decentralized Operating Management

General Motors believes very strongly in the use of internal competition to maximize efficiency and productivity among its division executives and managers. Therefore, it allows its division management as much freedom as possible, within corporate policy constraints, to guide their own operations. The local prerogatives afforded by this are normally quite extensive, and central staff is not allowed to intrude on division management unless absolutely necessary. Usually it requires an act of the executive committee or the board to override division management. Therefore, in dealing with this group, the central staff must use persuasive rather than authoritarian techniques to influence its decisions.

The freedom that GM allows its divisions today in regard to the configuration of products is, however, becoming more limited because of corporate standardization programs and federal requirements. For example, while Chevrolet has relatively complete control over the Chevette, it has much less to say about standard body configurations, such as the X-body, that are shared by other divisions. Certainly, any major change inviting standard components (such as the use of diesels, electronic fuel injection, or pricing strategy vis-à-vis other divisions) must be approved by the corporate product policy group.

Chevrolet, as well as the other divisions, conducts its own research programs, but these largely involve the adaptation of "corporate" designs to division needs rather than the development of new products.

*Separation of Product Policy Making
and Budgeting Powers*

In 1920 Sloan perceived the need to separate the power to finance projects, whether originated at the corporate or division level, from those people who advocated them. Under this doctrine all proposed projects that are approved by the executive committee (GM's top policy-making group) and require an allocation of corporate capital must be separately reviewed and approved by the corporate finance committee before being submitted to the board of directors.

Today, the executive committee and the finance committee are the most powerful decision-making groups at GM, yet they purposely hold somewhat adversary positions. General Motors still emphasizes the need for separate financial scrutiny of all new-product proposals because of the inherent risk in introducing new products into the automobile market, because of the limitations on capital, and because of GM's legal obligation to meet federal standards. It is possibly for this last reason that the company has placed responsibility for external relations (including government relations) under the separate auspices of the chief financial officer of the corporation.

Currently, the executive committee and the finance committee have four members in common: Thomas A. Murphy (chairman), Elliott M. Estes (president), Richard L. Terrell (vice chairman), and Roger B. Smith (executive vice president, financial staff). Murphy is chairman of the finance committee while Estes is chairman of the executive committee, which consists of the chairman and chief executive officer, the vice chairman, the president and chief operating officer, and the four executive vice presidents of the corporation.

Clearly, the four common members of both committees are key influencers in GM's strategic decision-making process. However, GM would consider the dual role held by these four individuals as a means of providing a necessary synergy between the two committees so that key decisions are viewed in the proper perspective, rather than as a means of steering approval by the finance committee, whose members also include six outside directors.

Committee or Group Decision Making
versus Individual Sponsorship

General Motors believes in and operates strictly through a committee system of decision making. While all programs and/or proposals are expected to have individual sponsorship, their approval is never determined by a single individual. The principal corporate committees/groups at GM involved in the product development process are shown in figure 17-1. They include:

> *The Executive Committee.* Determines which products/programs as well as priorities to recommend to the finance committee and the board.

> *The Finance Committee.* Establishes corporate financial goals and determines whether products/programs will receive capital funding before they go to the board.

> *The Product Policy Group.* Makes all basic decisions and recommendations regarding the development of standard corporate component hardware and engineering designs. This group also determines which new products can be commercially developed and distributed by which division. It also establishes and enforces corporate product policy regarding existing lines among the divisions. This group reviews the final configuration of a new product, including its price, promotion, and packaging. It is a large group, comprised of representatives from corporate management, research design, engineering and environmental activities, marketing, consumer relations, finance, purchasing, and manufacturing staffs, that actually designs, selects, and prioritizes products for approval. Final approval must be attained from the executive committee and the board, and capital must be authorized by the finance committee before a product is launched. In 1975 this group absorbed the former engineering policy committee. This committee, comprised primarily of the heads of division engineering and key people from engineering and research, tended to be a clearinghouse for all technical decisions, particularly those involving companywide products or component hardware. For example, decisions on retooling an engine plant to make diesels, front wheel drive, down-sizing of specific body sizes, and so on, were made by it.

> *Research Policy Committee.* Develops specific R&D policies and priorities in response to corporate goals established by the executive committee and the board, and reviews and recommends basic new technologies (for example,

new materials or processes) to the corporation. This committee deals primarily with untested, brand-new technological approaches.

The decision-making process within committees or groups is described as "consensus decision making." William Mitchell, GM's outspoken and recently retired vice president of design, noted that the product policy group sometimes toned down his department's designs too much. John Z. DeLorean, when he quit GM as vice president of the car, truck, and body group in 1973, stated that he thought the system was stifling. Despite the occasional slowness or conservatism of this approach, GM believes that it does help avoid major product blunders or missed opportunities.

While the committee or group decision-making system effectively helps GM screen out bad ideas and/or programs, it also gives impetus to good ones by encouraging creative thinking throughout the organization since the committees often hear presentations from individual sponsors from the divisions. Moreover, it is considered an honor to be invited to present an idea. If the idea is well received, division representatives are then expected to champion their concepts up the line. While this route is not meant to be easy, the system does encourage the development and communication of good ideas up to the highest levels of the corporation.

Systematization of Major Decisions

While GM encourages initiative and individual efforts, it discourages the personalizing of decisions or management functions. Some of the ways in which the company ensures that all critical decisions are a product of the GM system, and not an individual personality, include the following.

1. General Motors grows managers slowly within the GM system. General Motors staffs all key managerial slots from the ranks of experienced, proved GM executives and rarely hires from outside the company. The average length of service of all members of the executive committee, for example, is over thirty years, and the average length of service of the top forty-two officers of the firm is approximately twenty-nine years. The GM attitude is that an executive who makes it to a responsible position at GM will have been tested by the system and know explicitly how it works.

2. General Motors provides high incentive compensation to managers. The annual bonus could amount to two-thirds or more of an annual salary. Some outsiders believe that such incentives, combined with GM's deep-seated loyalty to its own, creates a basic "don't make a mistake" conservatism among longer-term corporate staff executives in particular. However, GM believes that such an approach, if performance-based and carefully woven into a system where

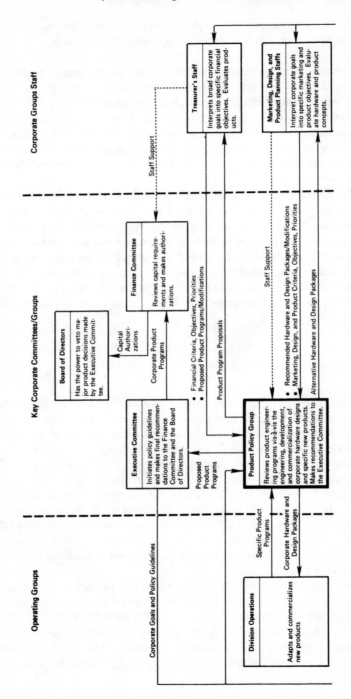

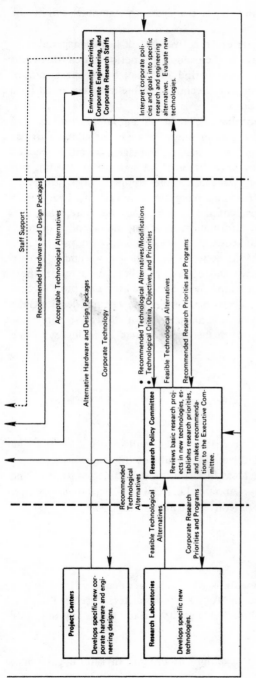

Figure 17-1. Framework and Process for Product Decisions at General Motors

incompetents are weeded out, encourages managers to compete within the ground rules of the organization.

3. General Motors purposely rotates executives out of key managerial roles periodically. A manager usually stays at the head of a functional area for two to six years. If not promoted out in that period of time, he or she is moved laterally. This prevents the function from becoming influenced too much by a single personality or an individual approach.

4. General Motors managers who have "plateaued" are rarely shunted aside into meaningless, unproductive roles, and incompetents are not allowed to rise to positions where they can cause problems. Instead, managers are either weeded out or told, more or less, that they have "leveled out." However, leveling out does not have a negative stigma at GM because the company does not try to "bury" people in the organization (incompetents are gotten rid of). Everyone is expected to remain a functional part of the system, and the system tends to work as it should, relatively free of informal maneuvering and crippling politics.

The climate created by these GM principles is one that encourages a balance between cooperation and competition, between individual goals and company goals, and between personal initiative and company policy. As a result, there seems to be just the right amount of team orientation and common purpose that is needed to make a collaborative style of management successful, despite GM's size. Ironically, while individualism or personal style is not allowed to determine decision making at GM, the entire GM management system is the legacy of one man.

Framework and Process for Product Decisions

Clearly, the GM product decision process is collaborative in nature and one where the ideas and initiatives of individuals are subjected to rigorous screening by several policy committees as the ideas filter up through the organization. The decision framework also includes appropriate checks and balances to ensure that all important corporate criteria and objectives are met.

Product Decision Framework

Figure 17-1 shows the general framework in which product decisions are made at GM. Central to this framework are the four key committees described earlier. Figure 17-1 portrays the relationships between important operating and staff groups and the committees.

Division Operations. In the product development process, division engineering, for example, will adapt a corporate product to its own particular needs. If it is a lead division, it will develop and test the product for the entire corporation. Buick, for example, is the lead division for the new V-6, turbocharged, "corporate engine." The product planning departments of individual divisions form particular product concepts or programs and promote them among the appropriate corporate committees.

While divisions do not make major product decisions without approval of the corporate product policy group, the executive committee, and the board, all project centers as well as key technical committees are staffed with division personnel. Because of this arrangement it is believed that the divisions still exert a great deal of influence over corporate policy.

Project Centers. Project centers are organized to optimize the development of specific products to be used by all divisions. (For example, there was an "A-Body Project Center" that essentially redesigned the down-sizing of the A-body for all divisions using it.) The project centers are perhaps the most significant change to GM's organization since the formation of the General Motors Assembly Division in the early 1960s. These centers are considered imperative to ensure GM's success in meeting government requirements in the 1980s.

The project centers report to a single individual, Charles J. Brady. Once a standard component or model design is completed by a project center, it is then passed along to division engineers for adaptation to each division's market needs. At that time the project center is disbanded.

Research Laboratories. The GM research laboratories perform all corporate research involving the basic sciences. Such advanced research might involve the design of a new, lightweight material or a revolutionary combustion or fuel metering process.

Corporate Staff Groups. These groups interpret broad corporate product policy guidelines into specific product/program criteria, objectives, and priorities. They then act as a jury for products and programs as they foment within the organization to ensure that the products meet the desired criteria, objectives, and priorities. The staff groups have a great deal of influence on committee actions and often prepare modifications or counterproposals to products being studied by the committees. The sort of decision criteria utilized by the staff groups includes federal standards, weight reduction objectives, marketability (for example, volume thresholds), cost per unit limits, after-tax return on investment, capital requirements, operating profit, design goals, failure rates, and any other specific objectives deemed important to the corporation. The biggest questions each new product or component must undergo at GM include:

1. Does it meet technical goals (for example, CAFE/SDEN standards)?
2. Will it provide an adequate ROI and operating profit?

3. Will it sell in the marketplace (that is, provide substantial volume)?
4. Will it allow GM to maintain car price increases below the general level of inflation?
5. Is it consistent with GM's overall product strategy?

Product Decision Process

While GM emphasizes that there are no hard-and-fast ways that decisions are made within the company, there tends to be a logical pattern in which basic product decisions are treated. In looking at figure 17-1 again, a conceptual overview of the way in which a product may evolve in the GM system can be seen. Briefly, the process begins with the establishment of broad policy guidelines and corporate goals by the executive committee. Such goals may include making a targeted return on equity, meeting all CAFE/SDEN standards on time, and continuing to lead the market in product quality and volume. It is then up to, say, the research policy committee, with help from staff groups, to interpret these guidelines and translate them into a set of practical research priorities and programs.

If basic research is not needed, the process may begin with deliberations by the product policy group on the reconfiguration or modification of an existing proved technology or product program. The down-sizing programs, for example, mostly began in this group. Programs to develop new, lightweight materials are still for the most part deliberated within the research policy committee.

A decision to establish a new lead division, or to allow a second division to develop its own product (for example, Chevrolet now wants to develop its own diesel engines even though Oldsmobile is currently the lead division), would very likely be made by the product policy group with help from appropriate staff groups.

The product policy group is currently the most important committee at GM below the executive committee with respect to the company's near-term product offerings. The group is influenced primarily by the product planning, engineering, and corporate design staffs; the treasurer's office; and division product planning staffs. The executive committee also strongly influences the product design process (via the establishment of corporate policy guidelines and goals) but does not actually develop specific product or engineering policies and priorities. This committee either screens out or gives impetus to specific product or corporate hardware proposals coming out of the product policy group, but the nuts-and-bolts decisions are actually made at staff levels, not in the executive committee.

The product policy group, which, as noted earlier, includes a cross section of representatives from various staff groups, has made some very critical decisions for GM. For example, as stated by one executive recently, "The down-sizing idea began by the executive committee gathering ideas in 1971, and in early 1973 the twenty-five person product group actually made the decision."

In the past, the product policy group tended to be dominated by design and finance. This was particularly true before William Mitchell, GM's well-known and outspoken design chief, retired. Since the early 1970s, however, many observers believe that engineering and finance have exerted more influence.

Key Decision Influencers

As already noted, GM does not have a formal strategic planning staff function. Among its divisions Chevrolet is believed to be the only one that annually develops a so-called strategic plan. Recently, the corporation has begun to develop a five-year plan, but this is believed to primarily relate to an economic forecast and pro forma capital funds projection.

Strategic decision making at GM, particularly as related to products, has always been an informal, team-oriented process, dependent more on the strength of the organization and its key players than on a formalized, written procedure. There is, however, a forward product planning group that provides a quarterly review of company strategic planning and long-range decisions. Paradoxically, even though GM people profess that there is no set way in which critical decisions are made in the company and, in fact, stress the informality of its decision making, GM's organizational philosophy and resultant management strength have developed from and contributed to an effective, rational process through which issues and problems have been successfully handled over the years, and have provided the company with a better track record than that of its competitors. In a sense, decision making at GM is a function of a unique corporate society, and it never varies greatly, regardless of the individual players involved.

Over the years GM has strived to achieve maximum consistency in the behavior of both its organization and its managers. In order to achieve the sort of consistency desired by Sloan and his successors, the company has resorted to some traditional patterns for staffing key management positions and for culturing managers that ensure a continuity of thinking. Table 17-1 presents a brief profile of some of the executives who are directly involved with current product policy decision making at GM. In scanning this list, it is easy to see some of the essential ingredients in the GM recipe for corporate policy making:

A GM/auto industry career orientation. As can be seen in table 17-1, key executives have worked their way up at GM, and most have had heavy division experience as well as staff experience.

Heavy emphasis at the top on engineering and finance. A GM tradition is to staff the chairman and chief executive officer position from finance and the

Table 17-1
Profile of Key Influencers of General Motors' Product Decisions

Name	Age	Current Position	Years of Service at GM	Experience at GM or Previous Experience	Education	Role in Product Decision Process
Thomas A. Murphy	63	Chairman & Chief Executive Officer	33	Accounting; finance	B.S., accounting	Chairman of Finance Committee; member of Executive Committee
Elliott M. Estes	62	President & Chief Operating Officer	32	Division engineering; general management	B.S., mechanical engineering	Chairman of Executive Committee; member of Finance Committee
Richard L. Terrell	59	Vice Chairman of the Board	41	Nonautomotive division management	Business	Member of Finance Committee, Vice Chairman of Executive Committee; corporate staff groups report to him
F. James McDonald	56	Executive Vice President (in charge of car, truck, body, and assembly divisions)	33	Manufacturing; division general management	General Motors Institute	Member of Executive Committee
Reuben R. Jensen	58	Executive Vice President (in charge of overseas operations—GMOO)	33	U.S. division engineering; manufacturing; and various general management functions including GMOO	B.S., mechanical engineering	Member of Executive Committee
Howard H. Kehrl	55	Executive Vice President (in charge of manufacturing and research staffs, patent section, and corporate planning group)	30	Research laboratories; division engineering; division general management	S.M, engineering mechanics	Member of Executive Committee, Research Policy Committee

Name	Age	Position	Years	Background	Degree	Committee/Responsibilities
Roger B. Smith	53	Executive Vice President (in charge of finance and external relations)	29	Finance; accounting	M.B.A.	Vice Chairman of Finance Committee; member of Executive Committee
Paul F. Chenea	60	Vice President, Research Laboratories	11	Educator; administrator	B.S., Civil Engineering; M.S. and Ph.D., engineering mechanics	Member of Research Policy Committee
David S. Potter	53	Vice President, Environmental Activities Staff	25	R&D; government service	B.S. and Ph.D., physics	Member of Research Policy Committee
Irvin W. Rybicki	NA	Vice President, Design Staff	NA	NA	NA	Member of Product Policy Group
F. Alan Smith	47	Vice President, Finance Staff	22	Finance; financial analysis	B.A., B.M.A.	Treasurer & secretary of Finance Committee; member of Executive Committee
Frank J. Winchell	60	Vice President, Engineering Staff	38	Engineer; engineering management	B.S., mechanical engineering	Member of General Engineering & Research Policy Groups, chairman of engineering Group
Lloyd E. Reuss	42	Chief Engineer, Buick	19	Engineer, product planning	B.S., mechanical engineering	Member of Product Policy Group
Robert C. Stempel	45	Chief Engineer, Chevrolet	16	Designer	B.S., mechanical engineering; M.A.; B.A.	Member of Product Policy Group
Robert J. Templin	51	Chief Engineer, Cadillac	31	Engineering; Special Assistant to President in charge of engineering programs	Degree, chemical engineering	Member of Product Policy Group
Robert A. Dorshimer	54	Chief Engineer, Oldsmobile	38	Project engineering; assistant chief engineer	Degree, mechanical engineering	

Table 17-1 continued

Name	Age	Current Position	Years of Service at GM	Experience at GM or Previous Experience	Education	Role in Product Decision Process
Stephen Malone	64	Chief Engineer, Pontiac	38	Chassis engineer; assistant chief engineer	B.S. electrical engineering	
Charles J. Brady	55	Director, Current Product Engineering Staff (head of GM project centers)	30	GM Proving Ground Director	B.S., mechanical engineering	

Source: 1977 Ward's Who's Among U.S. Motor Vehicle Manufacturers.

president and chief operating officer position from division operations and/or engineering.

Grooming and selection of top managers within GM as opposed to going outside. None of the executives listed in table 17-1 was hired into his present job from the outside.

Age/experience correlations. The average age of those on the executive committee is fifty-eight; the average length of service is thirty-three years. The average age of all others listed is fifty-three years; average length of service is twenty-seven years.

18 Toyota Motor Company

Overview

Toyota Motor Company (TMC) and Toyota Motor Sales (TMS) comprise "The Two Wheels of Toyota," each wheel revolving independently but both moving on the same axle. Toyota Motor Company is largely responsible for the manufacture and the research and development of automobiles; TMS carries out the related marketing and service functions. There is a strong sense of togetherness between the two, nurtured by a spirit of "Toyotaism" that derives from their common roots. Moreover, their relationship is the same kind of mutually cooperative relationship that characterizes Toyota's ties with its numerous affiliated parts and components producers, manufacturers of machine tools, and contract assemblers. This high degree of fluid interactions among the Toyota group of companies contrasts sharply to the closed nature of the company's dealings with groups or companies outside its own organization.

Toyota's basic character reflects Japan itself, a country where management and strategic decision making is the process of reaching a consensus. Moreover, the company's key leadership posts are held by direct descendants of its founders, and all members of the top management staff are highly capable experts in specific technical areas. Because of this technical expertise and the spirit of Toyotaism that has permeated the entire workforce, the Toyota organization moves with a deep sense of self-reliance and pragmatic conservatism. Although the company has adopted formal planning methods and planning tools, most of its actual decision making and planning are done in an informal fashion, primarily through joint policy committee meetings held at regular intervals to coordinate major policy decisions to be acted on by both TMC and TMS.

Attitude and Philosophy regarding Profits

Prior to 1974 Toyota, as well as the Japanese automobile industry generally, experienced high growth rates year after year. This fact, coupled with the company's light interest burden, the result of its strong aversion to resorting to debt, and its low dividend payouts (not unusual in Japan, but quite low by U.S. and European standards) enabled the company to produce sufficient profits and generate earnings required for capital expenditures. The prevailing philosophy at

161

Toyota, or for that matter at most large Japanese corporations, toward profits is that they should be sought in order to replenish the "trunk," and not be divided up for distribution to shareholders or as bonuses to top management since the trunk must grow in order for the corporation to continue to be viable, to compete successfully in the marketplace, to produce goods that satisfy changing consumer needs, and to provide employment.

This line of thinking prompted Toyota and other major Japanese corporations to seek growth through the enlargement of production scales and sales. As successive investments in more and more production capacity met full utilization, justifying further expansion, capacity expansion investments and profitability moved on in a self-perpetuating fashion. During the last few years investment priorities have shifted rapidly as investments in such things as emissions control devices have been required. In addition, because the market is approaching saturation, capacity investment has been a low-priority item, with the remodeling of existing facilities and equipment replacements taking its place as investment objectives for the purpose of gaining improvements in productivity.

The Onset of Five-Year Planning

Because of changes in the market as well as other developments in the external operating environment Toyota's attention to profitability is becoming more sharply focused. Whereas in the past planning largely consisted of developing quantified objectives in terms of demand projection, market share, and production volume, during the past couple of years objectives have been stated in terms of profit rates and rates of return and worked into Toyota's corporate five-year plan. Previously, TMC generally prepared its plan with a five-year scope in mind while TMS took a shorter view of only two to three years. Currently, both organizations are attempting to do five-year planning and better coordinate their individual plans and projections.

Although Toyota's planning will become increasingly systematized on a five-year basis, the company is apprehensive about rigidly committing to a plan extending over this period. Essentially, it is concerned about overcommitting to a plan based on future assumptions that may not hold true and thereby losing its flexibility to adjust to new or sudden changes in the external environment on which those assumptions are based. Toyota's awareness of this potential danger was awakened by the kinds of changes necessitated by shifts in political climate, economic realities, and public sentiments that led to passage of the U.S. Clean Air Act and its amendments.

Toyota realizes that in the past it has been more reactive than proactive to changes in the external environment. It is equally cognizant of the increasing pertinence of external influences on the company's strategic decisions. In order to improve the company's capabilities to closely monitor external factors and effectively evaluate their meaning to Toyota, the company is taking certain steps, including the establishment of an information-gathering office in Washington, D.C.

Product Planning and Development

Product development decision making at Toyota is done by a joint TMC-TMS committee that evaluates the design aspects and pertinent factors (such as U.S. regulatory requirements) which must be addressed. Toyota Motor Company contributes inputs related to technical philosophy, and TMS provides inputs on consumer tastes, marketability, and pricing. Together, they examine production cost, production volume, and marketability/price relationships. The product planning office at TMC initiates product design activities for a particular product development once the ideas for that product have reached a certain level of specificity. In parallel to these activities, the TMC technical planning office identifies from a long-term perspective the types of cars and automobile technologies that Toyota should be producing.

At Toyota the product planning and development process for a major remodeling effort or for a new-model project may require three to four years and cost anywhere from 10 billion to 30 billion yen. In the early stage of this process an evaluation of external factors and internal factors is undertaken. Basically, this involves the following.

External Factors

1. Analysis of trends in government regulations affecting the automobile industry, including exhaust controls and automotive safety requirements
2. Analysis of trends in the automobile market, including the projected vehicle's place in the market, the strength of competing vehicles, and consumer preferences
3. Analysis of trends in automobile technology, including trends in production and construction materials.

Internal Factors

1. Analysis of the manufacturer's technological capabilities, including the manufacturer's ability to design, test, and market the projected vehicle before the deadline
2. Analysis of the necessary investment in plant and equipment, the manu-

facturer's financial status, and the manufacturer's ability to undertake the investment

3. Analysis of the manufacturer's ability to make necessary preparations for production (that is, factory construction) in time to meet the deadline
4. Analysis of expected costs, taking all the above into consideration
5. Analysis of market competition between the projected vehicle and other vehicles currently being produced by the manufacturer
6. Analysis of quality improvements

The marketing aspect of Toyota's planning is done by the TMS business planning and market research section which produces one- and five-year plans. Demand forecasts for the Japanese and other markets are made, market research and analysis of customer tastes are conducted, and critiques of Toyota's current products in different markets are produced. Inputs to customer tastes and critiques of products are received from other sections involved in keeping track of warranty data and dealer comments. To a great degree the real function of the business planning and market research section is the coordination and consolidation of ideas, plans, and information coming from various functional departments. Toyota Motor Sales believes that because over 90 percent of Toyota's white-collar workers are college graduates, practically everyone in the company is capable of planning within his or her own function and should be encouraged to do so.

19 Nissan Motor Company

Overview

Nissan is frequently characterized by outside observers of the Japanese automobile industry as a highly institutionalized organization that emphasizes rational approaches. To the extent that this is true it is perhaps due to the fact that a number of people in key positions have banking backgrounds and the company has had nearly two decades of strong leadership under one person, himself a former banker. The recently appointed new president—a lawyer by training and with experience in marketing and finance at Nissan—is expected, with his frank and decisive personality, to enliven the organization and instill in it a spirit of aggressiveness and commitment to rise above Toyota.

The decision-making process at Nissan reflects the expressed wishes of the president regarding the overall direction the company should take. These wishes (directives) are generally not stated in numerical terms but, instead, have a very broad wording, such as "to exceed Toyota in exports within so many years."

The directors and general managers who head Nissan's functional departments, and who are equivalent in status to vice presidents in U.S. corporations, have the job of evaluating the implications of the president's goals and objectives for their particular areas of responsibility (such as exports, product, and finance) and provide their respective judgments and decisions. For example, for a company objective that involves exceeding Toyota's export performance, the financial department would conduct a financial analysis, and the export department would calculate the sales volume objective, and together they may conclude that it is necessary to expand a particular facility. These individual results and decisions are exchanged among the directors and general managers. A considerable amount of interchange follows to resolve any differences and conflicts, and all necessary adjustments are made. When a consensus is reached that every plan prepared by every department manager meets the president's announced goal, all the plans are assembled in a report submitted to the board of directors for approval. By this time there is a great deal of understanding companywide as to how each department will carry out its role, and the actual implementation moves smoothly and swiftly.

Nissan's decision-making process, like that used in most large Japanese corporations, involves a great deal of bottom-up decisions. The initial selection of a particular subject that requires a corporate policy decision originates at or below the middle management level. Analysis of this subject and the development of recommendations/conclusions are done within the group where the idea originated; whatever consultations are necessary with other groups and sections occur simultaneously. The combined results of all these efforts are then reported upward through several layers of the decision-making hierarchy to the top, requesting a corporate decision. Because of all the time and effort put into preparation at the earlier stages of this whole process, the passage upward through higher and higher echelons of decisionmakers increasingly becomes a simple process of obtaining approvals.

Capital Investment Decisions

In arriving at a capital investment decision, Nissan's finance department uses all the usual tools of financial analysis. The results of this analysis are fed into the report on which the company's decision is based. Although the ultimate decision on a particular capital investment project is not generally tied to a specific target profit rate, information on the projected rate of return is evaluated in conjunction with the other objectives associated with the project. (It is expected that Nissan will begin to give more weight and attention to rates of return—without sacrificing its objective of increasing market share—since the company is striving to improve its financial structure and because the era of emphasis on volume expansions has come to an end.)

Research and Development and
Engineering Decisions

Nissan's R&D and engineering-related decision making fully illustrates the process of decision making and consensus generation within the company. Eight directors hold R&D responsibility, and one executive vice president is in charge of production and R&D. These members hold weekly directors' meetings to discuss pertinent issues (for example, air bags). The general manager of the product planning and coordination department acts as secretary for these meetings. Minutes of the meetings are circulated to all departments in the company, thereby keeping individual departments and their respective general managers abreast of the proceedings.

The latest remodeling of the Sunny (B-210) demonstrates the bottom-up flow of decision making in R&D/engineering planning. In this effort product planning and coordination produced the original plan. This plan was then discussed with other departments and revised to incorporate their comments and suggestions. The resulting plan was then submitted to the board of directors for final approval.

Long-Range Planning

In its long-range planning Nissan uses a process similar to the one just described. Although called long range, the time horizon is generally three to five years—ten years is considered to be too long. The R&D department, the financial department, and several other departments as well as the company's long-range planning section participate in generating these plans. The long-range planning section is a small special staff housed in the president's office, which consists of two general managers, five managers, and five to six staff members. The business research department contributes inputs on the external environment—economic, competitive, and political trends. This department has one general manager, three managers, and a staff of thirty. Because all the departments submit inputs, the long-range planning section acts as both the coordinator of these plans and the link between the president and the various departments.

At times, when large issues or matters of special importance require decisions, ad hoc project teams are organized to study and report on them to the president. For example, about three to four years ago Nissan felt a need to clarify the company's long-range directions and, toward this end, created a project team for the specific purpose of long-range planning. The team has since been disbanded.

20 Honda Motor Company

Overview

Honda is frequently characterized as a company that takes a unique approach to everything it does, particularly when contrasted to most large Japanese business corporations where a hierarchical organizational structure patterns the decision-making process. Honda's basic character evolved as the firm catapulted itself from humble origins to achieve its current preeminence as Japan's sixteenth largest corporation under the strong personal influences of the founding inventor-adventurer, Soichiro Honda, and his vice president, T. Fujisawa. The fact that the approaches used by these two men worked so well is, to the company's current management, reason enough for retaining and fostering such approaches. This is particularly significant today when the company is under a trio of new top management and must forge a way to keep Honda a unique and exciting organization.

Honda considers flexibility, above all, as the company's most important value and the source of its basic strength. Organizationally, such flexibility is sought by combining the creative talents of specialized technical experts in an environment that facilitates the fluid, constant interchange of ideas and thoughts. At Honda, therefore, it is not managerial capabilities that are sought in the individuals who run the company but their specific areas of knowledge and their ability to pursue this knowledge further. Fujisawa, in retrospect, once conceded that both he and Honda would have been very mediocre managers in any other typical Japanese organization since they are technical experts in their respective fields, not managers.

This emphasis on individual technical expertise and a climate that facilitates the cross fertilization of ideas is reflected by the current leadership, consisting of the president and two executive vice presidents, as well as in the large open executive chamber where these three men and twenty-two other members of the board of directors (senior managing directors, managing directors, and directors) have their desks. The president has special expertise in technology; one vice president, in sales; and the other vice president, an engineer by training and a generalist by experience at Honda, is currently more or less responsible for the company's financial policies, even though there is no formal designation to that effect.

Management Structure

Since the joint retirement of Honda's two founders in 1973, the company's top management and decision-making structure has undergone a transformation whereby decision making is now more of a collective process rather than one where two individual personalities determine the thrust and direction for the company. The company's management structure has three levels. At the top is the board of directors, consisting of twenty-four company officers, including two supreme advisors, Honda and Fujisawa, and one outside member. Within this board is the senior managing directors' group, a decision-making body, consisting of the president, two executive vice presidents, and four senior managing directors. This group in turn controls three specialists' groups, each made up of managing directors and ordinary directors, and joined as the need arises by the heads of semi-independent affiliated companies.

The three specialists' groups are responsible for matters relating to "people, things, and money." While the individual sections and divisions responsible for day-to-day operations and for specific areas of profit making are under the supervision of the specialists' groups, the group members generally do not represent any section with daily responsibilities for profit. On major financial matters, such as bond or stock issues, the chief of the finance section works directly with the vice president in charge of financial policies for reporting to the board.

The specialists' groups are responsible for the company's new projects and, depending on the nature of the project, form an internal, ad hoc task force to study it. The three groups are represented so that views on matters relating to people, things, and money are all given expression and to ensure coordination among different intracompany divisions and subdivisions.

Even though the initial broad idea concerning the company's overall long-term direction may originate at the very top, decision making of specific varieties takes place at the middle management level. Consequently, the decision of any given ad hoc team receives automatic approval at the top.

The Strategic Decision-Making Process

There is a twenty-person corporate planning section within the Honda organization, but its functions are more in the area of corporate long-range strategies, the monitoring of ongoing projects, and maintenance of a publications library. The section also acts in an advisory capacity to the board.

An example of Honda's decision-making process which combines some systematic long-range thinking with the deployment of a task force is reflected in the company's choice in 1977 of Ohio as the site of its U.S. motorcycle (and possibly, at a later date, automobile) assembly operations. Approximately two years ago Honda's top management directed the company to look into the feasibility of U.S. production. Accordingly, a middle management task force was appointed by the board of directors to make a comprehensive study of transportation logistics, steel supplies, labor availability, and other factors, and to narrow down to several states the best potential candidates for location of the facility. These recommendations were reported to the top and approved. Subsequently, the team was given the task of identifying the best location, whereupon the Ohio site was selected. This choice was again communicated to the top and approved.

The company's current financial priority is to raise equity capital in a major way, including taking steps to tap the international money market. For example, prior to Honda's recent issuance of U.S. depository receipts in 1977, pertinent goals were set on such matters as growth rates, and these were communicated to the heads of every department and section. With regard to decisions relating to the company's capital spending programs, a directive may be issued from top management to evaluate a particular suggested program. The financial section examines the idea, analyzes its implications in detail, and reaches a conclusion which routed to the top for final approval.

Honda's system of developing new products and modifying existing ones is generated by three elements categorized as S (sales), E (production engineering), and D (development of new products and R&D). The company's recent decision relating to a new six-cylinder motorcycle was arrived at by the interaction of these elements, each advancing its arguments based on its own analysis of the potential, requirements, constraints, and so forth. The process of interaction of these three elements in reaching the final decision—or, for that matter, any interaction at Honda—is based on the principle of what the company character- izes as "mutual aggression." In other words, competing elements are strongly encouraged to pursue their individual positions all the way before the process of interaction produces a final balance among them. A similar principle is applied in seeking solutions to a given technical end, such as meeting a certain government regulation. The generation of alternative approaches is encouraged, and different subgroups of the R&D staff pursue multiple technical solutions in competition before the most appropriate one begins to surface. Honda believes that this approach is vital to the company's long-term technical proficiency and creativ- ity.

As inputs to the interaction process of the SED elements, the marketing section generates market projection data and the production engineering section determines the requirements for new plant facility and equipment. To determine what the consumer desires, Honda undertakes considerable research in order to develop products that reflect the results of this research. However, it is quick to point out that this is a process of trial and error. For example, in 1970 Honda introduced a 1,300-cubic-centimeter car model with considerable confidence since the company considered it to be a highly innovative and attractive product;

nonetheless, it suffered a bad market failure. In contrast, when introducing the Civic, despite the many solid engineering features in a little economy car, the company feared it had an unstylish look and would not sell well; the Civic instead became a popular seller. Not only did this car become Honda's staple volume-production model with potential for a long product life, but a growing number of similar-looking cars are now being produced by rival automakers. These include Ford's Fiesta, Mazda's GLC, and Mitsubishi's Mirage.

21 Volkswagen AG

Introduction

The following discussion of the decision-making process employed by Volkswagen focuses on strategic decisions—those management decisions that have a significant impact on the whole company and are not limited to one function/-department or one level of management; commit substantial corporate resources of personnel and/or capital; and address themselves to the (strategic) issue of whether VW is doing the right kinds of things, as contrasted to the operational issue of whether VW is doing things right (for example, most cost effectively). Using this definition, strategic decisions can be decisions with a long-term impact (such as decisions on new models or new production sites) or decisions with a short-term impact (such as pricing decisions or recall campaigns).

In the following attempt to characterize VW's mode of strategic decision making, emphasis is given to the formal (perceivable) aspects of decision making even though there are at least as many informal aspects (for example, the initial triggering of the process, the evaluation of decision alternatives, and decision criteria applied) as there are formal ones. This is because it is difficult, if not impossible, to assess the exact influences of the informal process. Focus is on the process itself, that is, how decisions are reached, not on the quantitative criteria applied (for example, ROI of x percent) or the results achieved (for example, profit or cash flow amount). The decision-making and planning processes will be discussed jointly, planning being the formalized, anticipatory decision process that commits corporate resources.

Prevailing Management Style

The manner of strategic decision making in an organization directly reflects the management style practiced. Thus, a good understanding of the management style is a prerequisite to understanding the process. Although German corporate law (*Aktiengesetz*) requires joint responsibility of VW's board of directors (a *Vorstand*-team approach) with the company's CEO acting only as *primus inter pares,* up to 1975 VW had very autocratic CEOs who personally made all major decisions themselves. For example, under Heinrich Nordhoff (1948-1968) all major decisions were personalized, and the organization reacted to the whims of the entrepreneur at the top. Kurt Lotz (1968-1971) personally made the decision to acquire NSU Motorenwerke as one of his attempts to diversity "at all costs." Rudolf Leiding's (1971-1974) first major strategic decision as CEO was to stop the costly Porsche development of a Beetle successor (EA 266) and concentrate all efforts on the VW Rabbit. This decision was apparently an intuitive one made by an informed engineer, not that of a general manager who consulted with functional experts in a systematic weighing of all the pros and cons of the decision.

As a result of this very centralized decision-making process in a large organization that operated in an increasingly complex environment, it has been rumored that VW's supervisory and management boards were often split on major strategic issues. Thus, when Toni Schmücker was appointed CEO in 1975, he saw as his priority task the closing of these rifts. Schmücker has been very successful in creating an effective management team by practicing a participative style of management.

Apparently, Schmücker will not make a decision himself. He typically asks his top executives to outline and evaluate the alternatives and to determine how *they* would proceed, and ultimately obtains a team decision, one that is understood and supported by the whole management board. This participative style of management has allowed more delegation of decision-making authority than was practiced in VW before. It has also necessitated an increased emphasis on more formalized, financially oriented decision making. For example, up to 1975 VW's export strategy was based more on a market share/market effectiveness assessment than on profit contribution. Schmücker, however, emphasized return on investment and return on sale, so that today a major criterion for assigning export delivery priorities is market profit contribution.

Organization of the Strategic
Decision-Making Function

To date, Toni Schmücker has not changed the very centralized Volkswagen organizational structure which, since 1948, has virtually remained the same. It is our opinion that in its endeavors to become a multinationally managed corporation, VW will probably change this structure within the next year. The following organizational units have primary responsibility for strategic decisions (see table 21-1).

The *supervisory board* has reserved for itself the final decision on major investments. Unique in Germany is a new clause in the corporate statutes which calls for the annual adaptation of a long-term plan (ten years) to be submitted to the supervisory board so that it can assess investment propositions in a corporate context. The supervisory board generally meets quarterly and more frequently when warranted.

The sales, production, purchasing, and other functions at VW—all headed by a board director—are each responsible for their own functional plans and

Table 21-1
Organization of the Volkswagen Decision-Making Function

Unit	Major Strategy Decision Functions
Supervisory Board (*Aufsichtsrat*)	Makes ultimate decisions on major investments; decides on board executive appointments
Management Board (*Vorstand* —the major strategy-making unit)	Makes ultimate decisions on product plans; approves corporate global plans (*Gejamt* plan) and budgets; decides on medium-sized investment proposals and prepares major investment proposals; decides on recall campaigns, major promotional compaigns, etc.
Product Strategy Committee (*Produkt Strategie Kommission*—PSK)	Prepares proposals for board approval on all strategic product issues (long-term model plans, short-term recall actions, etc.); decides on product plans submitted by the product planning committee
Product Planning Committee (*Ausschuss fur Produkt Planning*— APP)	Prepares, reviews, and updates product plans; prepares proposals for new developments (say, model improvements)
Planning Conferences	Corporate and functional planning staffs worldwide merger functional plans into corporate global plan

decision making. They have small central (functional) planning staffs that formulate functional strategies based on inputs from both the supervisory board and the corporate planning staff.

The *product strategy committee* is the most important source of strategic decision making within VW. Little is known to outsiders about this committee. It meets approximately once a month and is headed by Professor Fiala (responsible for RD&E). The CEO has only member status on this committee. Most of the issues dealt with by the product strategy committee are technical in nature (for example, introduction of new passenger safety devices and development of turbocharged Rabbit and Dasher diesel engines). Officially, the committee prepares proposals for board approval, but because all key decisionmakers (for example, the CEO and the directors of RD&E, production, and so forth) are members of this committee, it is *the unit within VW that has the most decisive impact on future strategy*. The product strategy committee by no means deals only with long-term issues; it deals with all product-related decisions that commit substantial corporate resources, including serious product-liability suits, recall campaigns, and so forth.

Because the product strategy committee only meets monthly and is viewed as a decision-*making* committee, its agendas are prepared by the *product planning committee*. This committee deals with more routine (operational) product planning issues and prepares and periodically reviews the product plans. Its members are executives from all functions who are usually positioned at the second or third level below the board—but the product planning committee reports directly to the CEO. This is due to the fact that Schmücker has reserved for himself the ultimate product planning decision authority. In essence, then, the product planning committee is more active in preparing product-related decisions than in actually making them.

Similarly, the *planning conferences* that exist at various levels of the VW organization are more important in preparing investment, product planning, and budgeting decisions than in actually making them. These conferences, similar to task forces, typically prepare decisions to be considered and acted on by the board.

Evaluation and Decision Criteria

As VW's decision-making process has become more formalized in recent years, the systematic application of financial criteria has become more decisive. Still, in terms of financial decision making, VW is not as tightly controlled a company as GM. For example, during many of his press conferences Schmücker has stressed that despite recent good results VW's ROS is still far from satisfactory. Also it is highly unlikely that VW would today repeat its "Mexican mistake" by establishing far too large a production facility in a country. In addition, financial criteria are applied in a flexible, nondogmatic fashion. For example, ex-VW executives claim that nonfinancial criteria, such as technical attractiveness, often play a significant role. These executives (one of them a former research manager) note that some technical proposals accepted by the VW board would not stand a chance at GM because of their low financial returns. [*Note*: This is a major reason why VW executives believe that the new generation of U.S.-made models will match VW products in size but will not be able to compete in technological content and quality. Apparently, the technical function (RD&E and production) has at least as strong an influence—if not a stronger influence—on product planning decisions as the controller function.]

In evaluating product and investment proposals, VW today uses a large number of financial criteria. Among these ROI and ROS play a dominant role for evaluating product and subsidiary plans. Cash flow and payback period are also used (but more sophisticated methods such as discounted cash flow are not).

Environmental Scanning

Volkswagen's strategic decision-making process is triggered by either intuitive recognition of strategic issues or systematic performance review/systematic environmental scanning to identify the threats and opportunities for the company. The intuitive approach is impossible for any outsider to analyze. It also plays less of a role in a participative style of management that emphasizes a decentralized and thus systematic approach to decision making.

At all management levels VW uses well-designed performance review systems that identify weaknesses and initiate corrective action. At lower levels of management, this involves routine budget reporting or product planning review. The management board gets a monthly planning and control report that includes a balance sheet and income statement (planned and actual data) and a large number of key ratios (cash flow, liquidity, asset turnover, ROS, and ROI).

Systematic environmental impact assessments, which are the basis for all long-term plans (subsidiaries and investments), are prepared jointly by the corporate central planning staff (total of 100 employees) and the functional department staff. For a company that is selling 2.2-plus million cars in 120 countries, environmental impact assessments represent a very complex task. In VW's attempt to systematize environmental assessments it has allocated responsibility as follows.

1. The *corporate planning staff* draws up scenarios as to the probable development of the economies in which VW has subsidiary operations—its projects' employment, gross national product, inflation, exchange rates, and so forth, mainly based on outside research institute reports.

2. The *functional department planning staffs* and the subsidiary planning staffs review and expand on these scenarios.

3. The *RD&E department* has set up a monitoring system for negotiating and assessing laws concerning automobile safety, emissions, and so forth. New developments are fed into the Wolfsburg data bank by the subsidiaries. They are then evaluated on the following scale:

Priority 1:   United States, Sweden, and Switzerland

Priority 2:   Other European countries (including Germany)

Priority 3:   Rest of the world (developing countries)

New regulations issued in the priority 1 countries initiate proposals for product modifications on new-product plans submitted to the product planning committee for review; decisions in high-priority cases go directly to the product strategy committee. We have not observed any attempts at VW to put the many expected environmental developments together on a worldwide VW group level and to formulate a group worldwide strategy based on their probable impact. Similarly, we have not observed a systematic assessment of VW's strengths and weaknesses performed at the group or even the subsidiary level.

Summary

Before Toni Schmücker took office, strategy formulation at VW was the prerogative of the CEO who shaped the group according to his concept of what the strategic posture should be. The relatively recent (since 1975) emphasis on decentralized decision making has resulted in an emphasis on strategic planning since, if an executive lower down the line is to have more decision-making authority, he has to know the overall strategic posture of the group.

At VW formal responsibility for strategic decision making rests with the management board. Of more practical importance, however, is the product strategy committee which addresses itself to all product-related strategic issues. Because this commission is, in effect, only a reduced management board, it can act quickly and thus exert the most significant impact.

Part V
Conclusions

22 Summary and Conclusions

1. *The regulatory process and pace are accelerating structural changes in the automotive industry, largely by magnifying traditional economies of financial scale. This is likely to lead to an increasing concentration of market share by one or two of the largest companies.*

Along with their intended benefits to the public in such areas as energy conservation, occupant safety, and emissions control, federal regulatory programs are changing the economics of U.S. automobile manufacture. The unprecedented acceleration of new-product development and the scope of effort required to create new generations of passenger cars that both satisfy regulatory standards and meet consumer needs have led the three largest U.S. companies to forecast capital investments of $43.7 billion over the next five years, double the amount invested by them in the previous five-year period.

The significance of the investment requirement is, in our opinion, threefold. First, it confronts Chrysler Corporation with three equally unattractive alternatives:[1]

To continue to attempt to offer a full line of products and to compete with the larger companies as it always has on a product line by product line basis. To do so, the company should be able to invest in new product development on a scale comparable to that of the largest companies, but it cannot.

To limit its product line to the intermediate and standard-sized vehicles that have normally tended to be the most profitable ones. However, a company that concentrates in these segments of the market is not likely to be able to meet CAFE standards.

To abandon the upscale segments of the market and limit its product line to compact and subcompact sizes. This would permit relatively easy compliance with CAFE standards but would make Chrysler wholly dependent financially on products that in the past have not generated, and in the near future probably will not generate, substantial profits for U.S. manufacturers.

Second, it places American Motors Corporation, a specialist in the compact and subcompact segments, in an even more precarious position than the one it currently occupies. The CAFE structure induces all the other domestic manufacturers to join AMC and the major foreign firms in what is apt to be a dogfight in these segments. Only significant participation in the compact and subcompact segments, even if only marginally profitable, would allow the Big Three to sell substantial numbers of more profitable, upscale intermediate and standard-sized cars.

Third, it will inevitably lead the financially weaker companies with thinner capital positions to develop their new product lines "on the cheap" or make them exceptionally sensitive to mistakes. Moreover, these companies will not have the financial capacity to correct any significant error in product development strategy. For them, every new product program is likely to represent a situation in which they will have to stake the future existence of their company, at least in its current form, on their ability to obtain reasonable success.

In these ways the regulatory framework has magnified existing differences between U.S. automakers by applying equally difficult standards to unequal companies. The smaller firms will either have to be unusually skillful or uncommonly lucky to reach 1985 with market shares and a product line breadth similar to those of the past. Without such skill or luck the regulatory framework will contribute to a considerably greater degree of relative industry concentration.

2. *The cost impact of regulatory standards, if passed through in automobile prices along with other cost increases affecting automobile production, is likely to create annual price increases that will exceed rates of inflation or growth in consumer income. If so, this may lead to the postponement of consumer auto purchases or to a "thrifting" of purchase patterns, either or both of which would diminish internal investment flows and thus adversely affect the capacity of U.S. automakers to generate the investment funds needed for regulatory compliance.*

During the past ten to fifteen years U.S. automakers have chosen to keep price increases below the level of increases in the cost of living and personal income. This was done in the expectation that it would help sustain high volumes of demand since purchasing behavior seemed more sensitive to these relationships than any others. A consequence of this policy has been a steady downtrend in their return-on-sales percentage. However, return on shareholders' equity has largely been sustained during this same period by a relative decline in new capital investment and by volume growth.

Apart from regulatory-related costs, the major cost pressures on U.S. automakers are the following:

Labor expense. In addition to triennially negotiated basic increases in wage levels and benefits, contracts with the United Automobile Workers include an "uncapped" cost-of-living adjustment.

Phantom productivity. Contracts with the UAW include a 3 percent annual "improvement factor" for productivity gains. There is some doubt as to whether auto industry productivity has been actually increasing at this rate.

Suprainflationary inputs. These would include energy and energy-intensive raw materials that probably represent one-third of total manufacturing cost.

New costs. Prominent among these are direct cost increases associated with product liability and recalls and the indirect expense of attempting to minimize both.

Each of the major future regulatory cost increments—passive-restraint systems, three-way catalytic converters and their electronic control systems, depreciation, and amortization associated with increased fuel economy investment levels—is large in itself, and together they will "clump" in a short time. If passed through in pricing, along with the cost pressures enumerated above and any other aspects of inflation itself, they would probably result in a more notable series of price increases than any in recent times.

Two concerns flow from this. First, consumer perception that car prices are rising more rapidly than personal income, especially without any consumer-perceived counterbalancing benefits, may lead to the postponement of purchase decisions. The degree to which this concern is justified is difficult to evaluate. Certainly, Volkswagen sales in the United States declined sharply in the early 1970s as the prices of Volkswagen cars increased rapidly. In the past six months, U.S. prices of most major Japanese cars have increased approximately 15 percent, but consumer response is not yet clearly formed. However, in a typical recession auto sales do tend to move disproportionately downward as auto prices and consumer income expectations diverge.

Second, if purchase decisions are not postponed or reach the point at which they cannot be postponed any longer, consumers may choose to shift their purchasing toward smaller cars or less luxurious versions of larger cars. Because neither is commonly very profitable for U.S. automakers, a tendency of this sort toward a "thrifting" of the market would diminish the flow of funds required by U.S. automakers for their 1978-1985 investment programs.

3. In the event of initial consumer resistance to new vehicle configurations, price increases influenced by regulatory costs, or CAFE-related product-mix goals of U.S. manufacturers, the marketing capabilities of the automakers can probably succeed in counteracting some resistance, but efforts to counter major resistance may result in a shrinking of profit margins and, with this, a shrinking of internal investment flows.

The use of conventional marketing tools, especially consistent advertising in high volume, appears to have been an effective means of inducing the public to accept moderately novel configurations to which there has been some initial resistance, such as the new down-sized General Motors A-body vehicles. Any deep-seated resistance or major obstacles are more unyielding to the marketing tools available to the automakers and require tools that diminish profit margins. These include dealer incentive programs, special accessory "package" promotions aimed at the public, and dealer rebates. In the most extreme situations direct rebates to purchasers have been utilized.

It is unlikely that the automakers will find it desirable to deploy their marketing resources to stress occupant safety. There seem to be ample indications, both in survey data on interest in passive restraints and willingness to pay for them and in the use of existing safety devices, that the mass of the public is relatively indifferent to this sort of appeal. Because the impact of federal Motor Vehicle Safety Standard 208 will fall more or less equally on all automakers, promotion of this standard is unlikely to figure prominently in their marketing efforts.

On the other hand, even though public interest in fuel economy seems only moderately greater than interest in occupant safety and is diminishing from 1974 levels, U.S. automakers are likely to actively promote the fuel economy levels of their subcompact and compact vehicles for two reasons. First, they must sell these vehicles in substantial volume as the "price" of being able to also sell higher-profit, upscale vehicles under the CAFE structure. Second, in promoting their new smaller cars, fuel economy is a "hard number" that can be used to demonstrate competitive advantage.

4. *Even a minor recession in the next eight years is likely to destroy the abilities of Chrysler and American Motors to maintain their announced investment programs to meet already established regulatory requirements. A major recession, comparable to that of 1974-1975, or a second minor recession prior to 1985, would lead General Motors and Ford, between them, to raise approximately $5 billion of new capital simultaneously in a capital market of shrunken capacity. As a point of reference, the largest U.S. corporate borrower, AT&T, has never raised more than $1.569 billion at a single time.*

Based on the capital investment estimates made by the Big Three in June 1978, it appears that their total capital investment for the eight-year period from 1978 to 1985 will amount to approximately $69 billion, about half of which we calculate to be associated with regulatory compliance. Under more or less normal circumstances with respect to profit levels, dividend payout rates, amortization, and depreciation (and assuming no strikes, economic recessions, or major unexpected changes in the economics of automobile manufacturing or consumer behavior), General Motors would probably need about $1.0 billion more in investment capital than it generates internally, and Ford would need slightly more than half that amount. Under such circumstances neither requirement should pose major difficulties for either firm. Chrysler, however, would need to obtain approximately $1.25 billion of incremental capital over and above its internal generation. It would have to be able to repeat its current capitalization effort (preferred stock and warrants) once again before 1982 and obtain additional borrowed funds on the strength of its augmented shareholders' equity.

If a recession of half the relative magnitude of 1974-1975 intervenes (and it is difficult to imagine any continuous eight-year period without at least one moderate recession), General Motors and Ford, although seriously affected, should be able to meet their capital needs through their internal reserves and perhaps some medium-term borrowing. The impact on Chrysler of even a modest recession might be catastrophic, forcing the company to begin to dispose of marketable assets or to abandon some product lines.

A second moderate recession of this same sort would confront GM and Ford with the need to collectively generate $5 billion in external capital to replace lost profits. To place this figure in context, it is four times more than the largest amounts the two firms have ever raised at any one time. Ford's portion of it would be approximately $2 billion. The largest single borrowing ever undertaken by AT&T, a company with five times the assets of Ford, was a debt issue of $1.569 billion floated in the 1970 recession and costing that firm an interest rate of 8.75 percent, the highest it had ever paid. A $5 billion joint requirement would almost certainly place pressures on the capacity of the capital markets when those markets are likely to be suffering from capacity limitations.

Two relatively moderate recessions or one recession of the magnitude of 1974-1975 would contribute greatly to a much higher degree of concentration in the U.S. automobile industry and would significantly alter the financial structures of the nation's first and third largest manufacturing entities.

5. The length of the product planning cycle has stretched to five or more years by the organic character of change required to meet regulatory requirements. Despite the efforts of the automakers to delay "point of no return" decisions as long as possible in the cycle, they are nonetheless making many basic decisions without the sort of confidence that a closer-in view of consumer interests and behavior would provide. This increases risks, especially for the smaller U.S. companies that cannot absorb any major product errors.

The product planning process typically begins with an effort to identify consumer interests and to integrate these with such business objectives as profitability, volume growth, and improved market share. The cycle, however, has grown progressively longer since each succeeding new-product program is technically more complex than its predecessors. The cycle now requires at least sixty months for a new product that does not embody unusual new technology and may stretch to seven years if extensive new technology is required.

This creates two major impacts, one affecting all companies equally and one primarily impacting the smaller and/or less financially strong firms:

All firms. The longer lead times present in the product planning cycle and the organic character of the new products being developed creates the possibility that shifts may occur in consumer behavior to which new-product programs cannot be adjusted because aspects of those programs must be "frozen" before such trends become visible.

Smaller, financially weaker U.S. firms. To the degree that the new-product development cycle permits, the larger automakers can pursue at least some parallel alternatives. The smaller companies do not have the financial resources to do this to the same extent. In a sense this forces them to interpret consumer needs even farther away in time than the largest firms and naturally increases the likelihood of misinterpretation.

6. *Current trends in the tort litigation system, working on the high expectations likely to be aroused by compulsory passive-restraint systems, will cause a considerably higher frequency of product-liability suits to be launched against the automakers and, very likely, a higher product-liability related cost. The magnitude of this incremental cost remains virtually impossible to forecast.*

Although the treatment of product liability differs in the fifty different U.S. jurisdictions, in the past decade there has been a growing shift away from the concept of manufacturer negligence toward one of strict liability. As this has occurred, defenses of abnormal use, assumption of risk, and contributory negligence have been diminished. According to Professor Richard Epstein of the University of Chicago Law School, a widely acknowledged expert in liability law, the tenor of the times is in favor of the plaintiff's recovery with the burden of proof on the defendant.

This change in the interpretation of liability has been accompanied by the retroactive application of new interpretations. In addition, some jurisdictions are permitting the awarding of punitive damages.

The passive-restraint systems to be implemented under MVSS 208, no matter what their degree of actual reliability in performance, are likely to arouse even higher levels of performance expectation. Because of the technical limitations of both air bags and passive seat belts, we believe that these expectations are likely to generate a high frequency of litigation. This appears to be already foreshadowed by the 1976 experience of General Motors in its ratio of lawsuits to air bag deployments. Concern about the unpredictability of the air bag product-liability risk has been cited by Eaton Corporation as a principal reason for abandonment of its air bag program.

The uncertainty present in the rapidly shifting definitions of liability in many states presents a variety of issues in which risk forecasting becomes uncommonly difficult. The following are just a few illustrative hypothetical instances:

The owner of a car equipped with a passive seat belt system is injured and claims the use of deficient technology (that is, the choice by the manufacturer of belts rather than air bags) because of the resultant cost saving.

The owner of a car equipped with an air bag is injured, primarily because that person did not affix the lap belt, but nonetheless claims manufacturer liability.

The owner of a car equipped with a passive-restraint system disconnects the system, is injured, and claims manufacturer liability on the grounds that the system should not have been so easy to disconnect.

Although passive-restraint systems will generate fewer bodily injury claims, they also seem certain to generate many more product-liability claims. Without major changes in the tort litigation system of the sort proposed by the Department of Commerce Interagency Task Force on Product Liability, the financial impact could reach massive proportions and hold broad implications as an issue of public concern.

7. *Despite the dependence on a single technology (three-way catalytic converters) to meet 1981 emissions standards, despite dependence on the Republic of South Africa as the primary source of the catalytic metals, and despite a mismatch between the natural occurrence of the metals and proportional requirements for them in the converter, it does not appear likely that either the technical or the political problems involved will interfere with the ability of the automakers to meet 1981 standards.*

Despite continued research by U.S. automakers to find substitutes for the three-way catalytic converter, largely maintained because of their interest in either lowering the cost of emissions control equipment or diminishing their vulnerability to cartel pricing initiatives, a practical alternative does not appear to be in the offing.

Of all the countries producing platinum, rhodium, and palladium, only South Africa and the Soviet Union have them in sufficient independent quantities (that is, other than as by-products of nickel or copper extraction), and only South Africa is a supplier that, in the past, has maintained continuity of offering and contract pricing.

Although ruptures in relations between the United States and South Africa or internal civil disorder in that country is a practical concern, stockpiles other than the strategic one maintained by the U.S. government for capital goods industries are estimated by metals experts to be large enough to meet one to two years of auto industry consumption. Given this forecast, it would appear that the U.S. auto industry could weather any sort of short- to medium-term interruption in the supply of catalytic metals from South Africa.

Once the generation of cars equipped with three-way catalysts begins reaching scrappage in 1981, the United States will be capable of recovering an estimated 40 to 80 percent of the metals through a recycling program. The major immediate concern appears to be a higher requirement for rhodium in relationship to platinum than occurs in natural ores. Extensive research is underway on this problem.

Note

1. Since this report was drafted in June 1978, Chrysler announced plans (on August 10, 1978) to sell all its European car and truck manufacturing operations to P.S.A. Peugeot-Citroën of France for about $426 million in cash and stock. Chrysler's chairman, John J. Riccardo, and its president, Eugene A. Cafiero, in a letter to stockholders, stated that one of the major effects of the sales would be to allow Chrysler "to focus more of its resources on the North American market" and to complete the company's "most extensive plant-modernization and product-renewal program" in its history.

Appendix A
Some Relevant
Aspects of Regulatory
Issues Impacting the
Japanese Automotive
Industry

The following topics are briefly discussed: safety, emissions standards and diesel cars, fuel economy, and noise.

Safety

Safety issues in Japan peaked around 1970 when 16,700 deaths and 900,000 injuries were attributed to motor vehicle traffic accidents. In response, traffic rules enforcement activities by the police agency were tightened, improvements in safety-related features of vehicles were required of the automakers, and the number of safe driving training programs was increased. Partly as a result of these efforts, accident figures have since declined visibly to the point where safety is no longer the dominant public issue it once was. By 1977 the number of deaths and injuries recorded was 8,900 and 600,000 respectively. In that year the number of registered motor vehicles was 32 million. The 1977 accident figures respectively correspond to the injuries' figure ten years earlier when the number of motor vehicles in operation was only 10 million units and the deaths' figure of 1958 when only 1.7 million vehicles were in operation.

A breakdown of deaths statistics for 1970 and 1975 is:

	1970	*1975*
Automobile drivers/passengers	5,612	4,013
Motorcycle drivers/passengers	2,941	1,696
Bicycle riders	1,940	1,254
Pedestrians	5,939	3,732
Others	333	97
Total	16,765	10,792

Japan's Ministry of Transportation implemented the country's first five-year motor vehicle safety plan in 1972. Patterned closely after the U.S. motor vehicle safety standard, the Japanese plan covered eighty separate items, including the installation of active seat belts. By 1978 some 70 percent of these items had been standardized. A second plan is currently being deliberated, again covering approximately eighty items similar to those on a list published by the U.S.

National Highway Traffic Safety Administration. A technical council consisting of industry representatives, scholars, and government members was slated to complete a study of these items and make recommendations about regulatory details by the end of June 1978. It is generally believed that this second plan, when finalized, will not mandate passive-restraint systems but designate this item for study as a long-term potential regulatory option.

In Japan pedestrian safety is currently of greater concern than vehicle occupant safety. In fact, a pedestrian safety issue involving large trucks has recently been under debate at the national Diet (the Japanese parliament). A lowering of the driver's seat, a broadening of the range of vision, and control of overloading practices are some of the safety mechanisms that may be required by the time the debate is concluded.

As for vehicle occupant safety, the use of air bags is generally only in an experimental stage so that no discussions on them have taken place. Moreover, air bag technology in Japan has not advanced to the level of U.S. air bag technology. Consequently, if the United States requires the use of this safety device, the Japanese automakers who market their automobiles in the United States may have to import this technology from abroad. Meanwhile, within Japan the position of the Japanese government is to attempt to educate the public about the merits of using active seat belts. If occupant safety becomes a major public issue, the government's initial move will be to step up its campaigns to promote their use. At any rate, the current primary concern of consumer groups is neither air bags nor seat belts, but rather the problem of rusting.

In the event that Japan does not mandate passive-restraint systems while the United States adopts such requirements, there is some chance that the Japanese Diet may eventually be prompted to require them in Japan as well.

Emissions Standards and Diesel Cars

The Japanese government has completed the implementation of emissions control standards for passenger cars with respect to three pollutants. In 1978 the standards at 0.25 gram/per kilometer for hydrocarbons, 2.10 grams/per kilometer for carbon monoxide, and 0.25 gram/per kilometer for nitrogen oxides. (These are equivalent on a per-mile basis to 0.41 gram, 3.40 grams, and 0.40 gram, respectively.) Because the Japanese test procedure is less stringent than the U.S. procedure in terms of the driving cycle applied for taking measurements, Japanese cars in compliance with Japan's 1978 standards would register larger emissions under U.S. testing.

Although current sales of diesel cars are still nominal, the merits of these cars are beginning to be recognized by Japanese consumers, and some optimistic industry estimates predict sales of 250,000 to 400,000 units annually within the next year or two. In addition to Nissan, which had been producing diesel cars for some time in a very limited number to cater to a small corner of the taxi market, since 1977 Toyota and Isuzu have added diesel versions to their model lines. Industry observers predict that two other automakers may soon follow suit. The largest diesel import brand in Japan is Volkswagen, and the popularity of the diesel Rabbit is such that there is reportedly a six-month waiting list for delivery.

The Japanese government has kept the diesel fuel tax at a much lower level than the gasoline tax, primarily because of the wide use of diesel engines in trucks. This has kept the price of diesel fuel approximately 30 percent lower than the price of gasoline. In addition, because the fuel consumption of the diesel is about 30 percent lower than that of the gasoline engine for distance traveling, these two factors, in combination, amount to the fuel cost of a diesel car being 50 percent that of a gasoline car.

Despite the new interest in diesel passenger cars, there is considerable uncertainty as to how emissions control regulations for this category of car might develop. Today, diesel cars are grouped with trucks under the existing regulations. Some tightening of emissions control standards will take place for this group in 1979 with few technical problems expected. But if any further tightening is undertaken, the chance of diesel cars' clearing such requirements with the current technology is felt to be slim.

Thus far the potential environmental issues of diesel passenger cars have not surfaced because of their insignificant number. However, if they increase in popularity and, as a result, their volume rises significantly, it is quite possible that pressures may grow for the government to tighten emissions control requirements and bring them closer to the levels that are applied to gasoline cars and to regulate other problem areas associated with diesel car technology.

Fuel Economy

Japan's energy problems are acute because of her nearly complete dependence on imported petroleum to satisfy her energy requirements. Still, per capita energy consumption in Japan is comparably modest for such an industrialized country. This is probably explained by the fact that the tight energy situation has always been a strong presence, and because the rise in Japan's standard of living has been only a relatively recent phenomenon. This is reflected, for example, in the small average size of cars produced in Japan; the tax structures that are graduated against larger and more powerful cars; and, mainly because of Japan's dense land-use patterns, the relatively short average distance that a car is driven in a year.

Nonetheless, the fact remains that energy issues are of vital concern to Japan, a matter that has becomeall the more apparent since the energy crisis. The fact that recent increases in the value of the yen have contributed to a relative decline in the prices of imported materials, including petroleum, does not alter the country's heavy dependence on foreign energy sources.

Currently, the Japanese Ministry of Transportation conducts fuel economy tests on all automobile models (ten-mode testing at an average of 60 kilometers per hour) and publishes the results. In general, the fact that the country's gasoline consumption volume is within the natural proportion of the petroleum products mix with which crude oil is refined into gasoline and other types of fuels has helped the automobile sector avoid becoming a focal point of the government's attention. Even so, there is a chance that the government's involvement in automobile-related energy issues will probably increase in coming years, as well as the already considerable level of consumer awareness of the cost-saving advantages of energy-efficient products.

Within the Ministry of International Trade and Industry there is an energy agency that is currently formulating a national energy policy with the goal of reducing Japan's energy usage by 10 percent by 1985. As part of this goal various fuel-efficiency requirements could become defined and even legally forced on different energy-using sectors, including the automobile. Fleet fuel economy requirements are, therefore, a possibility. The secular trend in the Japanese automobile market has been the upgrading and up-sizing of the average automobile produced and bought, a trend that is expected to go on. The Ministry of International Trade and Industry is watching this with some reluctance and, if it goes on too much longer, may find it reason enough to begin considering some government regulatory measure.

Noise

The denseness of land use in Japan makes noise-related nuisances a significant social issue. The automobile industry believes that if strict truck noise standards are enforced by the government, such requirements will make serious demands on the industry that will probably be more difficult to implement than the recent emissions control standards. Thus far the 1979 standards are designed to reduce the permitted noise level from the current 92-decibel level to an 89-decibel level, which is equivalent to the European level. Considerable difficulties are anticipated by the industry if these standards are tightened further. According to one estimate, a lowering of the level by only 3 decibels would probably require a halving of engine size. Encasing the whole engine would be an option, but this would generate new problems relating to engine heat, vehicle weight, and access to the engine for repair work.

Index

About the Authors

John B. Schnapp, director for this book, is a vice president of Harbridge House, Inc. He holds a B.A. with high honors from the University of Pittsburgh, has done graduate work in international economics at the University of Rochester, and is a graduate of the Advanced Management Program at the Harvard Business School. Since joining Harbridge House in 1966, Schnapp's consulting activities have been primarily focused on national and multinational corporate management, economic analysis, international trade and policy formulation, marketing management, and international development programs. Recent Harbridge House studies of U.S. and foreign automobile manufacturers directed by Schnapp have examined industrial relations policies, R&D strategy and management, the major influences of the imported automobile industry on the U.S. economy, and the impact of the current fuel economy regulatory structure in terms of public policy needs. The results of each of these studies were used as the basis for corporate strategy development or government policy decision making.

Jennifer Cassettari, research coordinator for this book, holds a B.A. from Brandeis University and a master's degree in library science from Simmons College; she also attended the Urban Education Program at Wesleyan University. Cassettari has coordinated the research activities for a number of Harbridge House studies, focusing on such areas as automotive research and development, the government-business interface, and auto property claims systems. Her recent activities include an extensive data-gathering and analysis effort in order to prepare a monthly automotive industry newsletter, research support in an economic analysis of the imported automobile industry, and preparation of a report and the development of expert testimony for hearings before the International Trade Commission in conjunction with charges of "auto dumping."

Patricia A. Comer holds a B.A. from Regis College; ADA Certification from University Hospital, University of Michigan; and an M.B.A. from the Wharton School, University of Pennsylvania. Since joining Harbridge House in 1977, Comer has specialized in the areas of transportation planning and policy, market analysis, strategic planning, cost analysis, and financial management. Currently, for the Transportation Systems Center of the U.S. Department of Transportation, she is project director for a two-year effort to monitor worldwide trends in the automotive industry and to report these in monthly newsletters and quarterly reports. Other recent efforts include the direction of an automotive product-liability study, a distribution and marketing strategy analysis focusing on dealership organization and a consumer research effort, an analysis of air freight costs of shipping seafood and fresh fish to various U.S. markets, and an interstate comparative analysis of electromechanical and computerized toll collection systems.

Juergen Lange is a vice president of Harbridge House and director of the Harbridge House Frankfurt office. He studied at the Stanford Graduate School of Business, holds the U.S. equivalent of an M.B.A. from the Free University of Berlin, and attended the European Institute of Business Administration (IN-SEAD) at Fontainebleau. Since joining Harbridge House in 1966, Lange has directed consulting, research, and management development projects for leading international companies throughout Europe as well as the United States. Specializing in the areas of planning, organization, marketing, financial analysis, and Common Market legislation and policy, Lange has recently participated in the development of profiles of two U.S. automakers on behalf of a European automobile exporter considering a joint venture with a major U.S. automobile manufacturer, assisted various British and German companies wishing to invest abroad, and presented management training programs for various companies in the automotive and electronics industries.

J. Frank Remley, III, is a principal of Harbridge House. He holds a B.S. from Princeton University, an M.S. from Stanford University, and an M.B.A. from Boston University. Remley joined Harbridge House in 1969. Since that time he has specialized in economic and financial analysis, marketing, and long-range planning and policy studies, providing analytic consulting services to top management in both government and industry. His most recent activities have included coordination and management of a major national two-day transportation conference on the future of freight systems technology for the director of the Transportation Systems Center, U.S. Department of Transportation; participation in a rapid transit study to provide data and guidelines to assist government decisionmakers faced with the responsibility of designing policies on the allocation of capital investments for urban transportation; an assessment of the feasibility of changing the toll collection system used by the New York State Thruway Authority; a management audit of the Southern Connecticut Gas Company; and a study of a potential merger between two public utility companies in Vermont.

Hiroko Sakai, a senior associate of Harbridge House, holds a B.A. from Wellesley College and an M.A. and a Ph.D. from Columbia University. As a specialist in transportation planning, economic analysis and multinational business, Sakai has participated in numerous Harbridge House projects since joining the firm in 1972. Most recently, she directed a study to assess the technological, financial, and consumer/product impacts of CAFE standards for passenger cars as a mechanism for dealing with public policy needs. Her other activities have included a study to investigate practices and experience with the use and characteristics of automobiles in foreign countries, an intensive microview study of the Japanese automobile industry, an investigation of the impact of imported automobiles on the U.S. economy and the U.S. consumer, a strategic planning conference on the government-business interface dealing with the Japanese experience, a determination of the feasibility of an integrated industrial complex and identification of the most economically viable combination of industries for the complex, and the development of freight-flow modeling and traffic volume projections for various transportation/shipping consulting assignments.

Jan-Hendrik van Leeuwen, a Harbridge House consultant, holds a bachelor's degree from Lausanne University in Switzerland, a master's degree from Leiden University in The Netherlands, and an M.B.A. from the Harvard Graduate School of Business Administration. Since joining Harbridge House in 1976, van Leeuwen has specialized in the areas of international marketing, law, and economics, providing consulting services to clients in both the United States and Europe. Recently, he directed a study of a broad range of location alternatives, binational management issues, organizational issues, and facilities and budget alternatives for a major Japanese automaker interested in setting up a U.S. advanced styling studio. In addition, he directed the update of a study that documented major influences of the imported automobile industry on the U.S. economy. Other activities in which van Leeuwen has been involved include a study of the economic, judicial, and political impact of compulsory licensing in Europe; a study of traffic management and energy conservation measures in West Germany, Belgium, and The Netherlands; and a feasibility study of a proposed investment to develop and market a new domestic car incorporating both domestic and foreign technology.